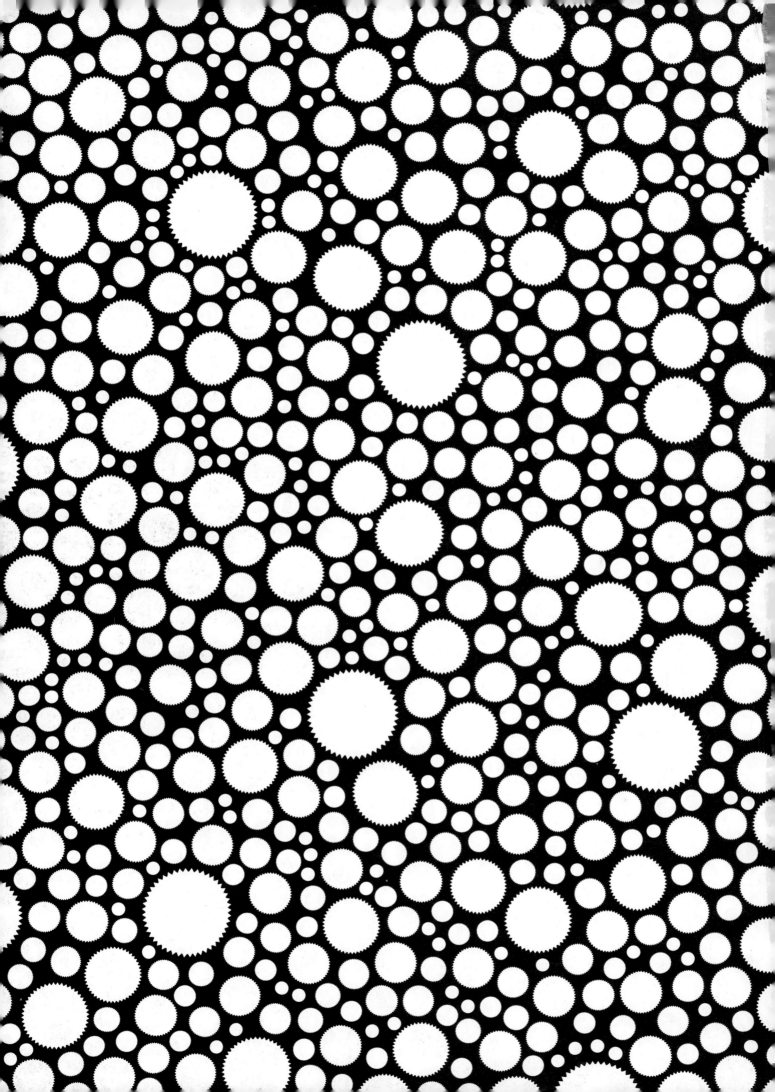

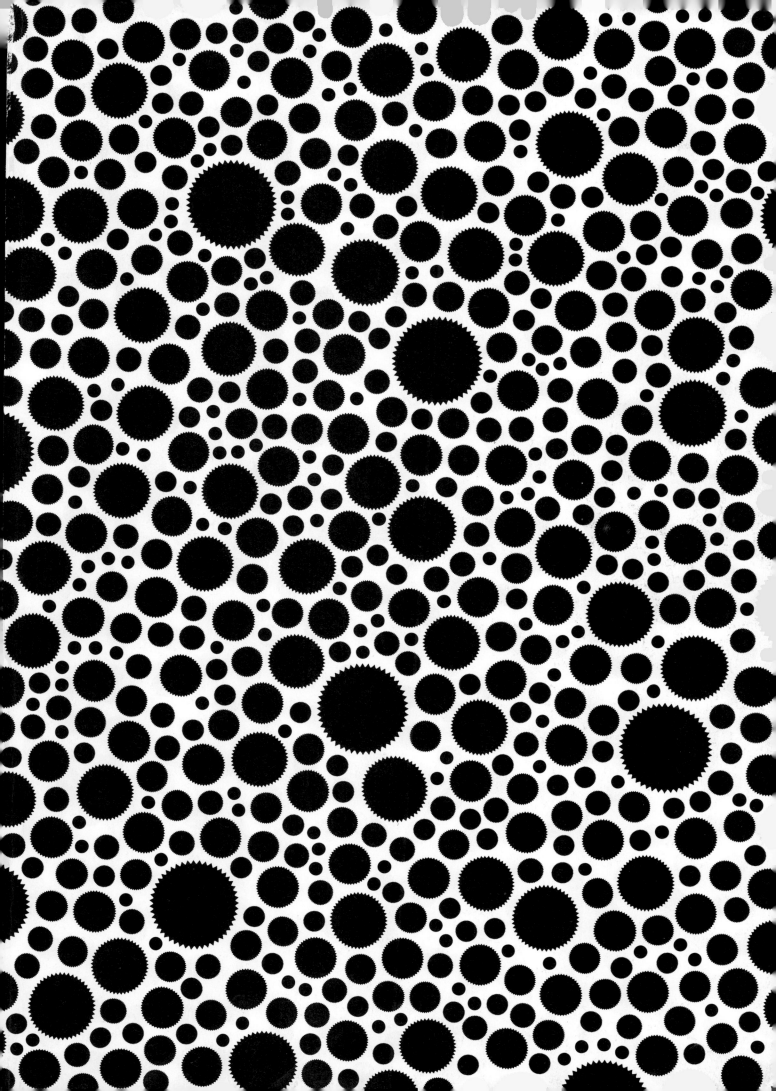

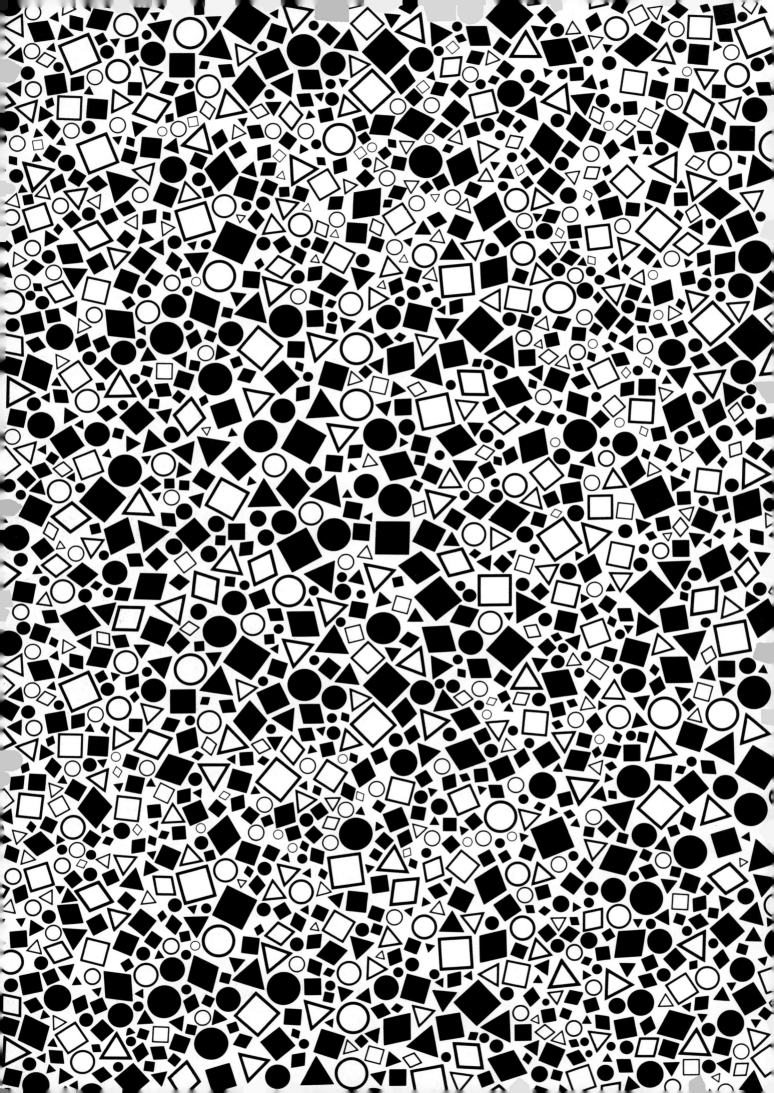

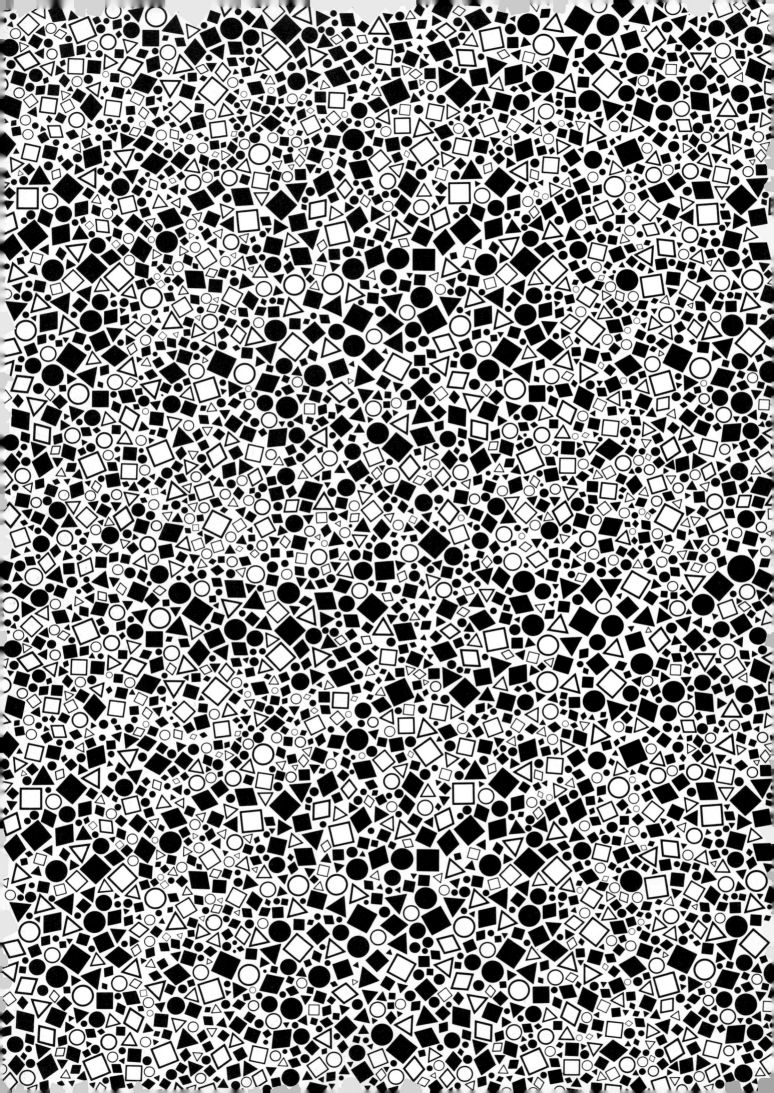

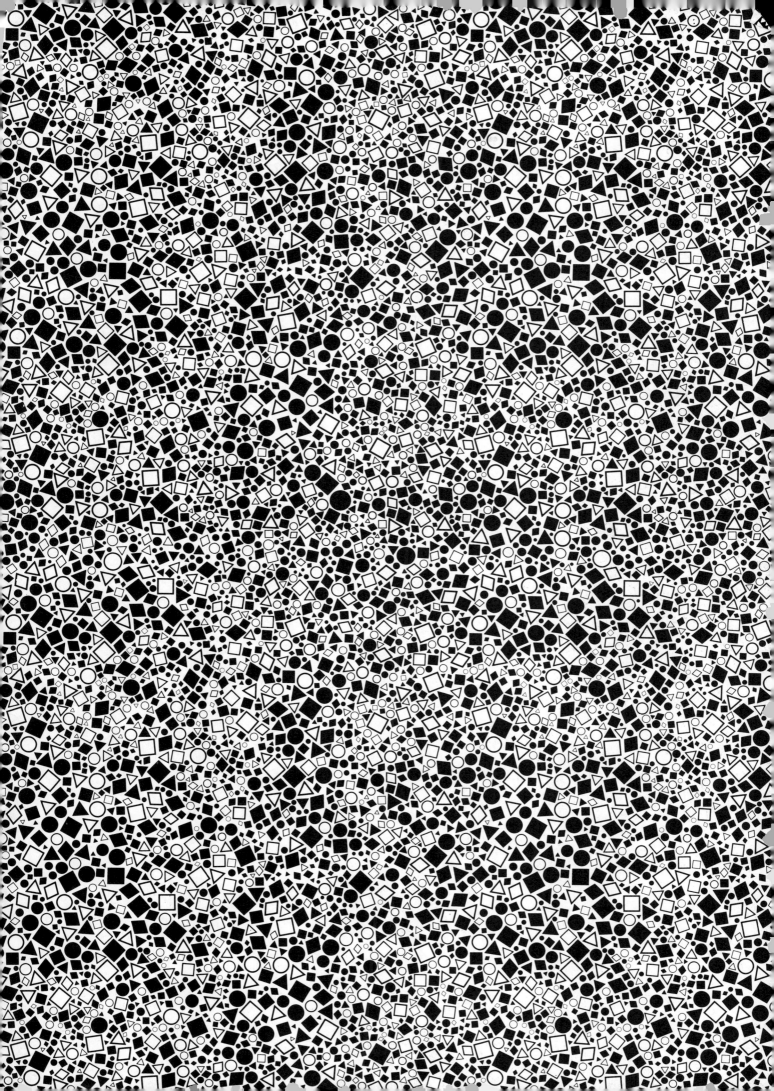

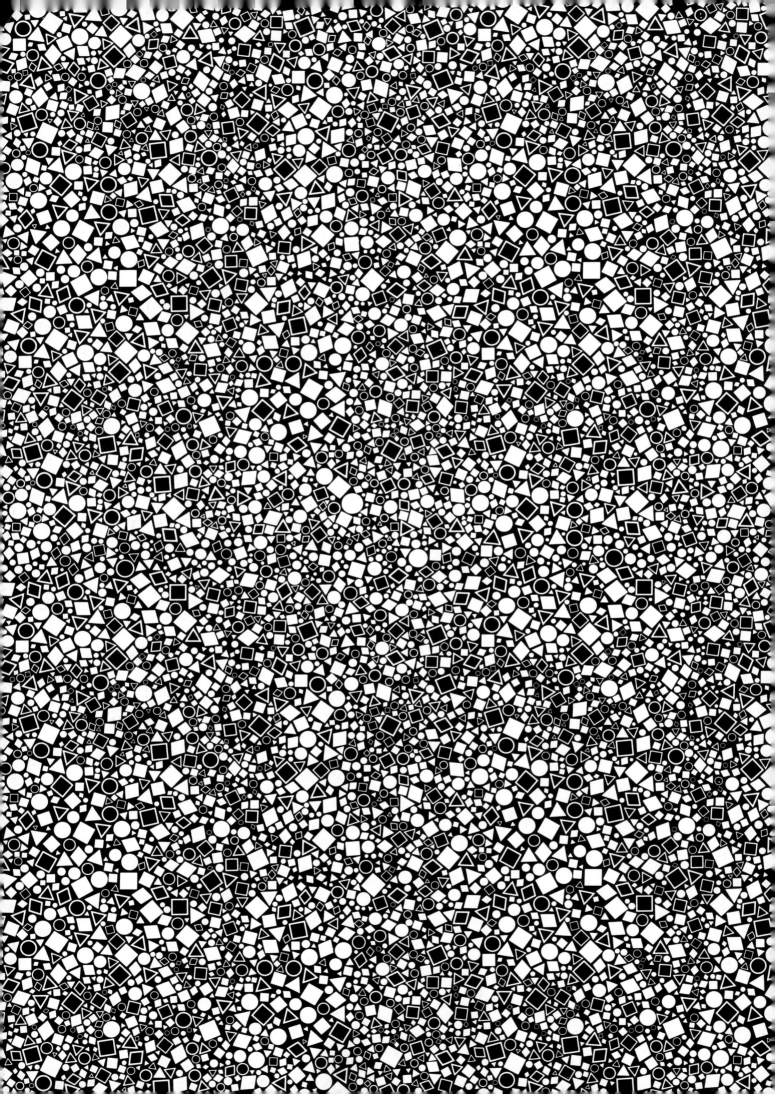

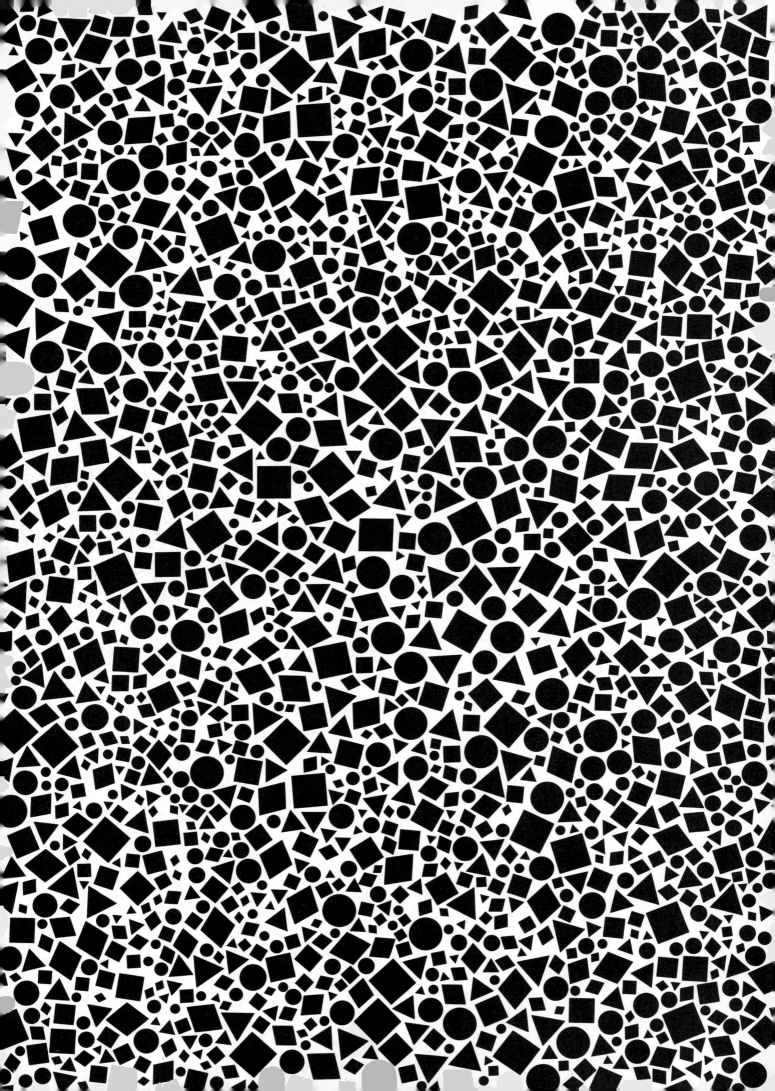

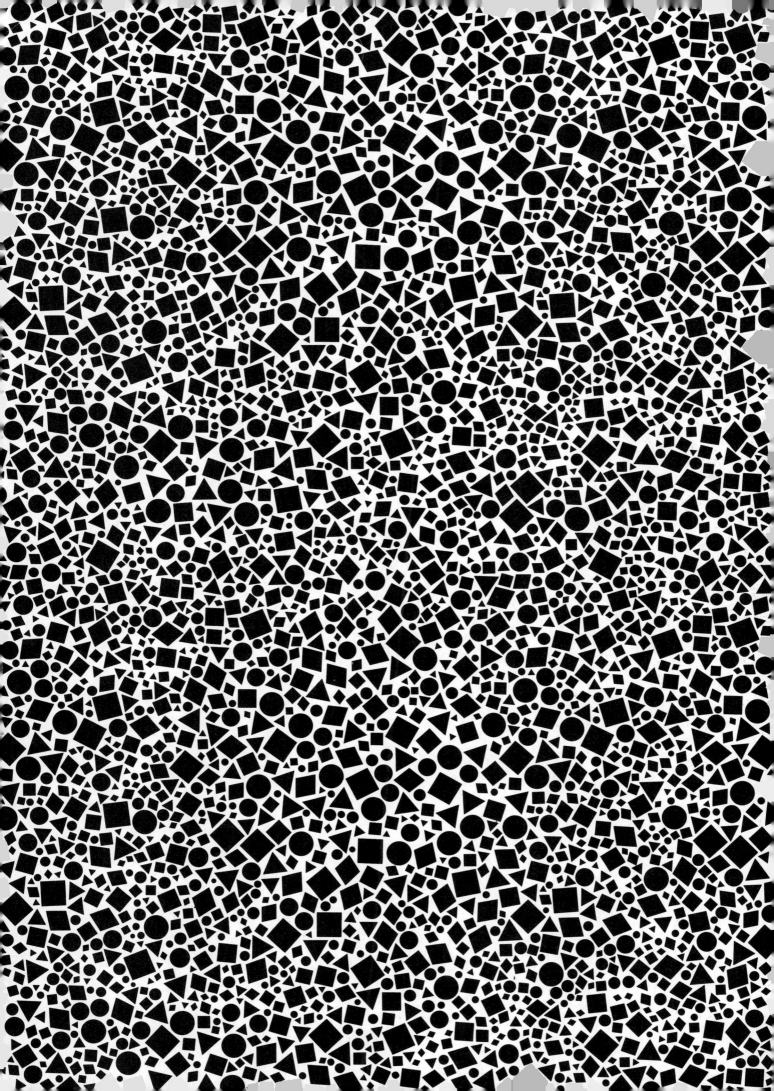

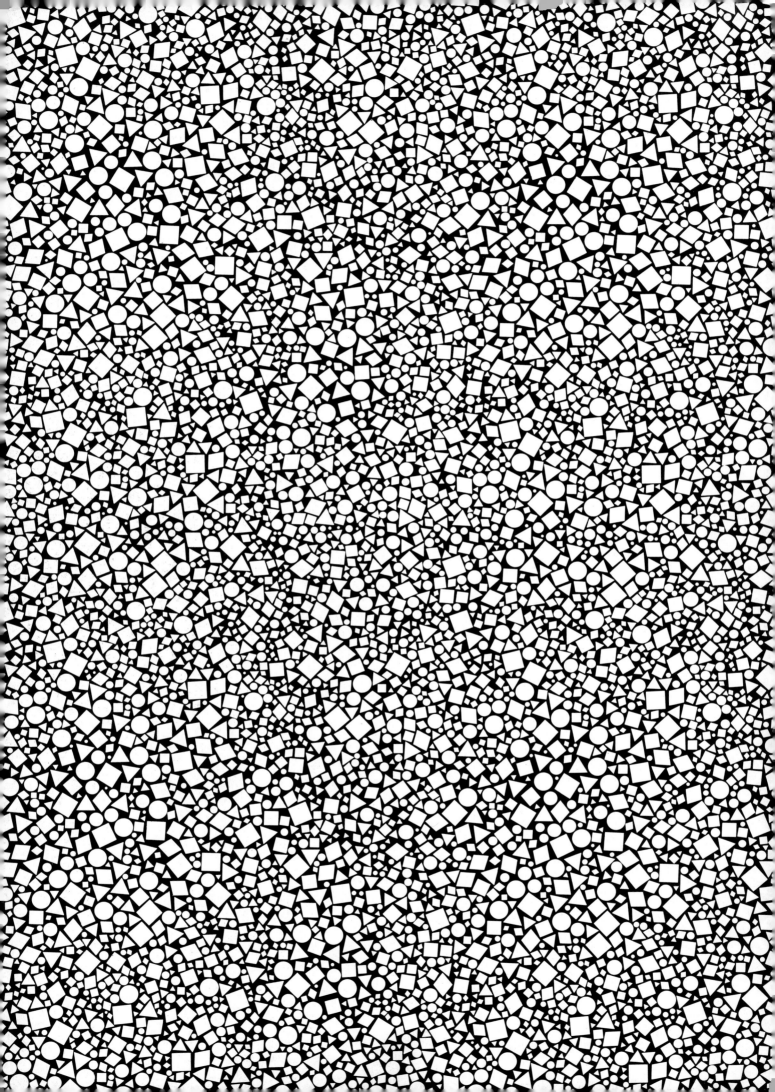

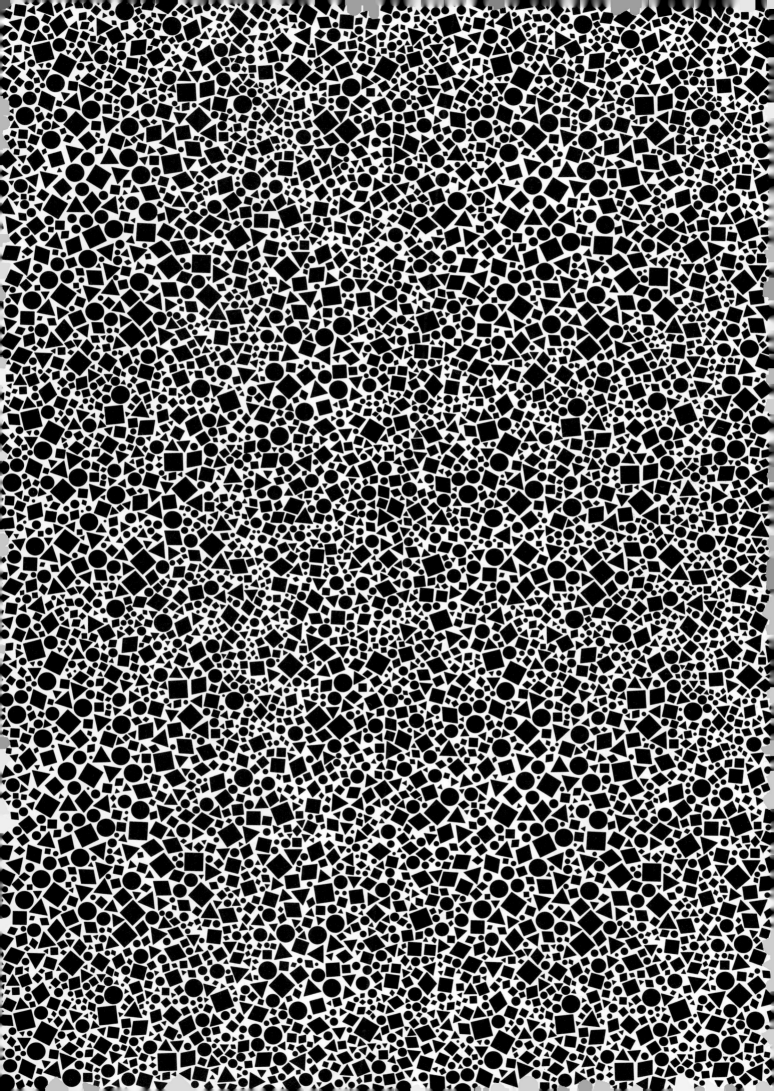

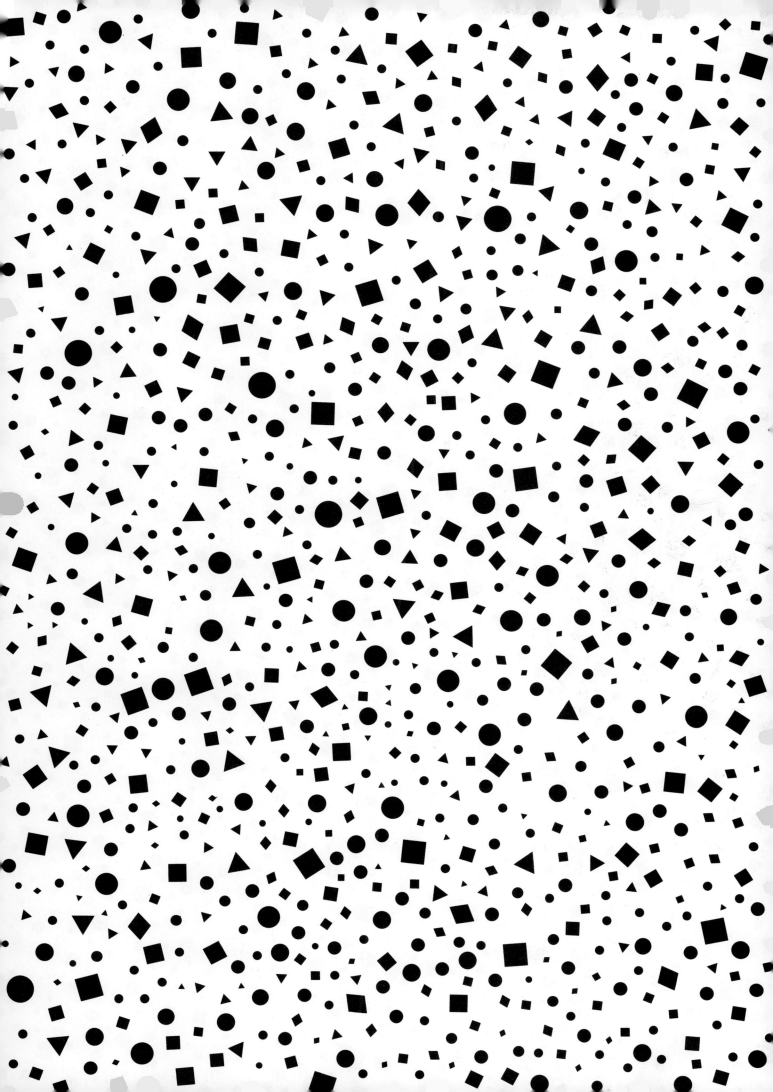

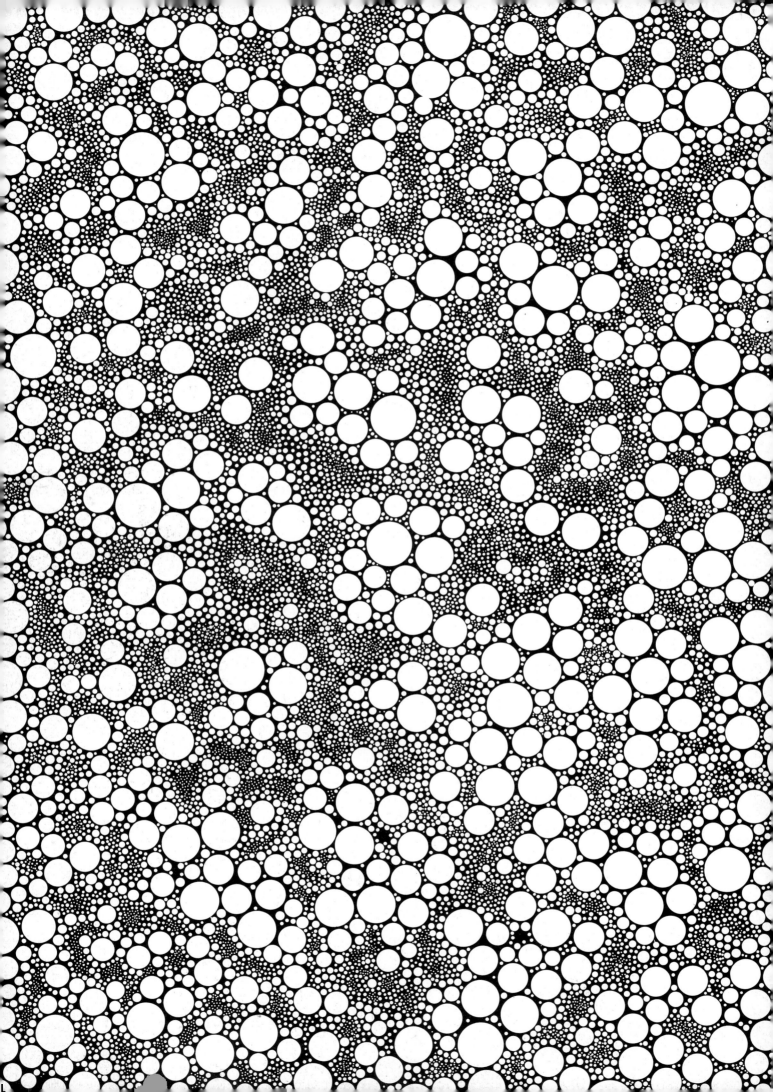

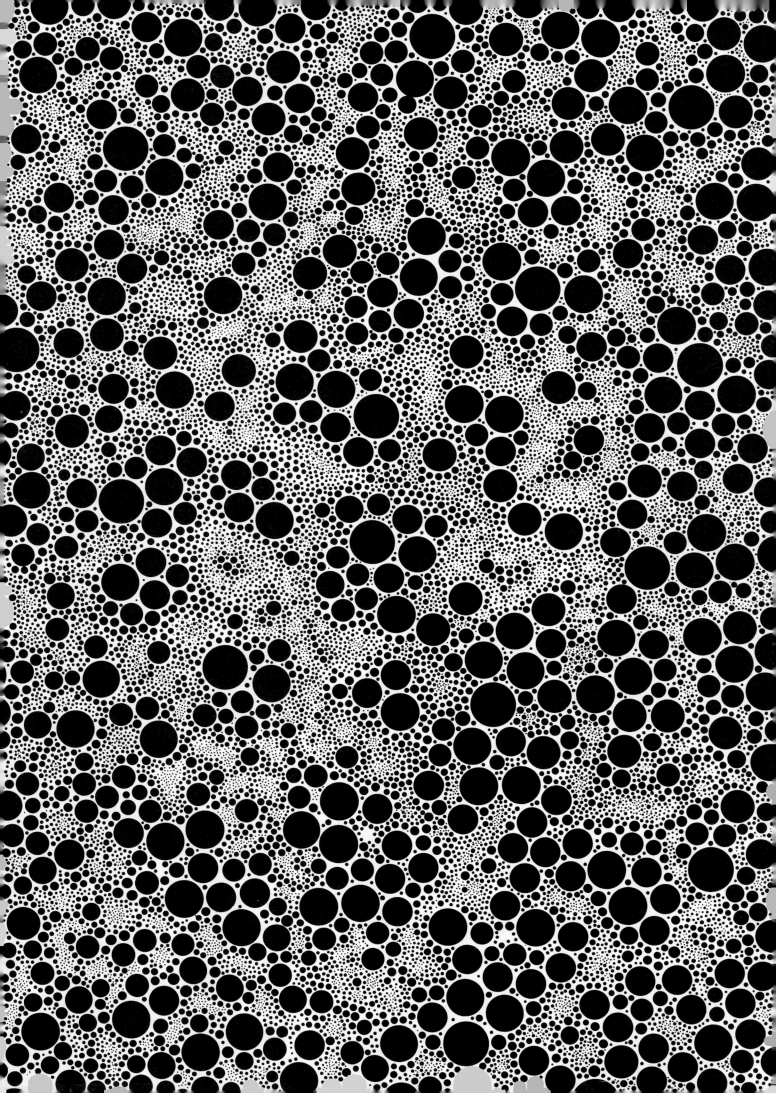

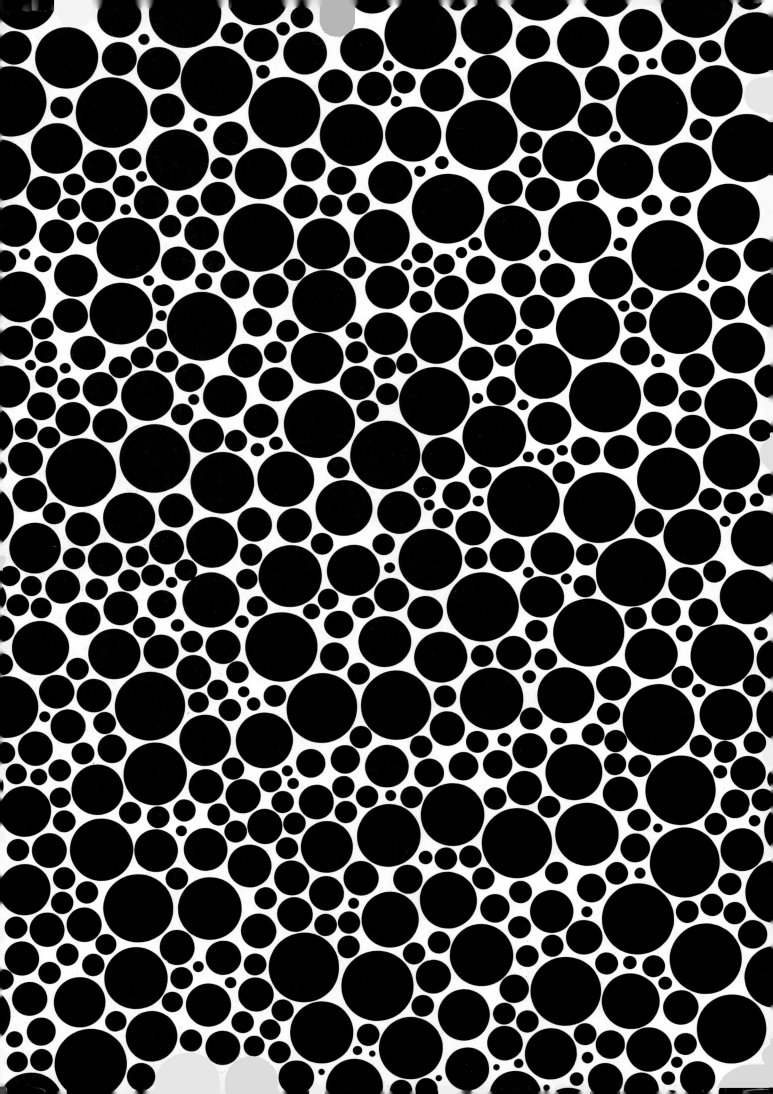

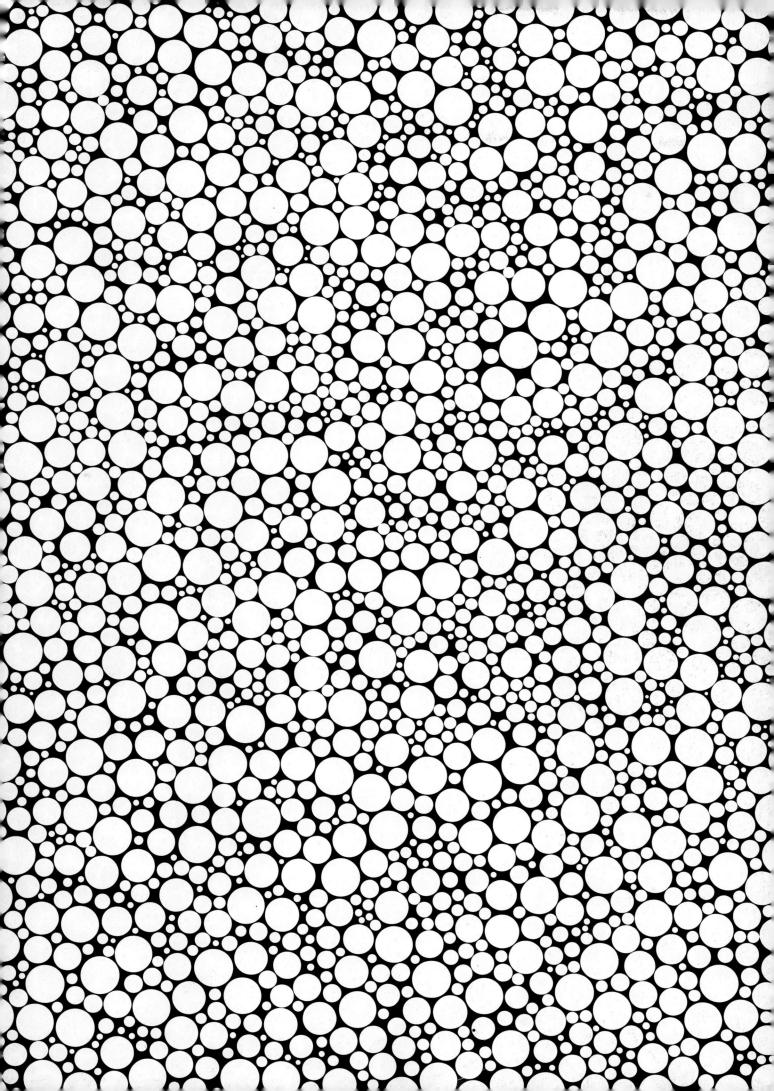

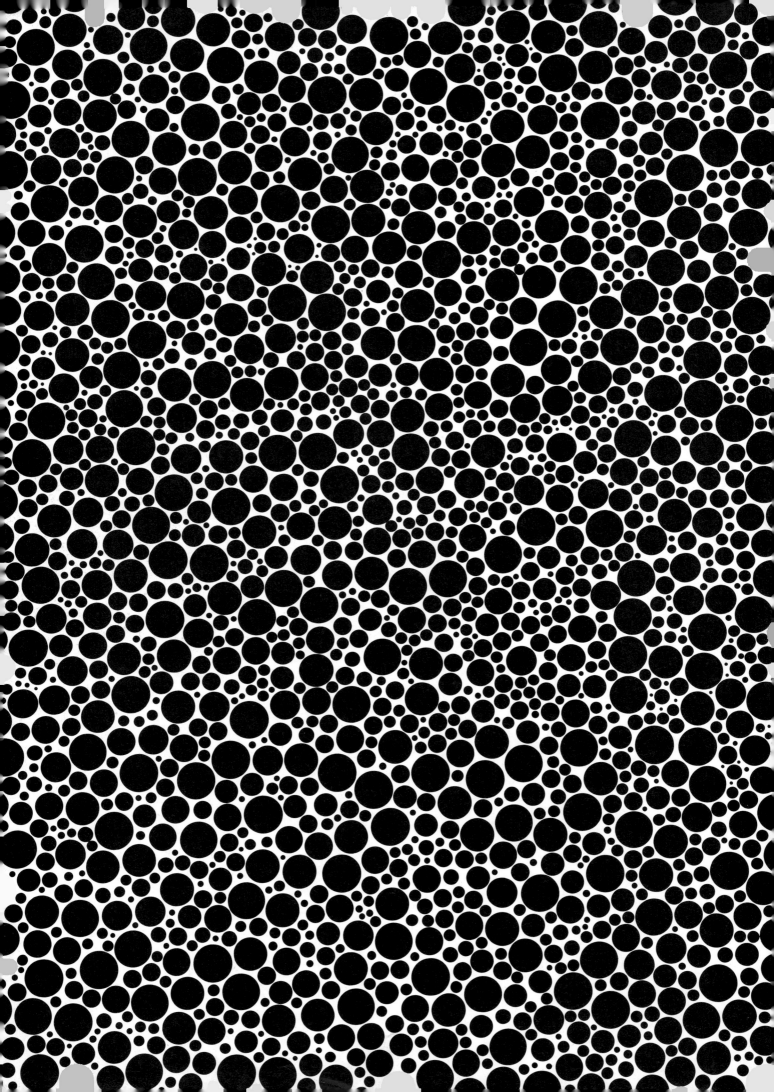

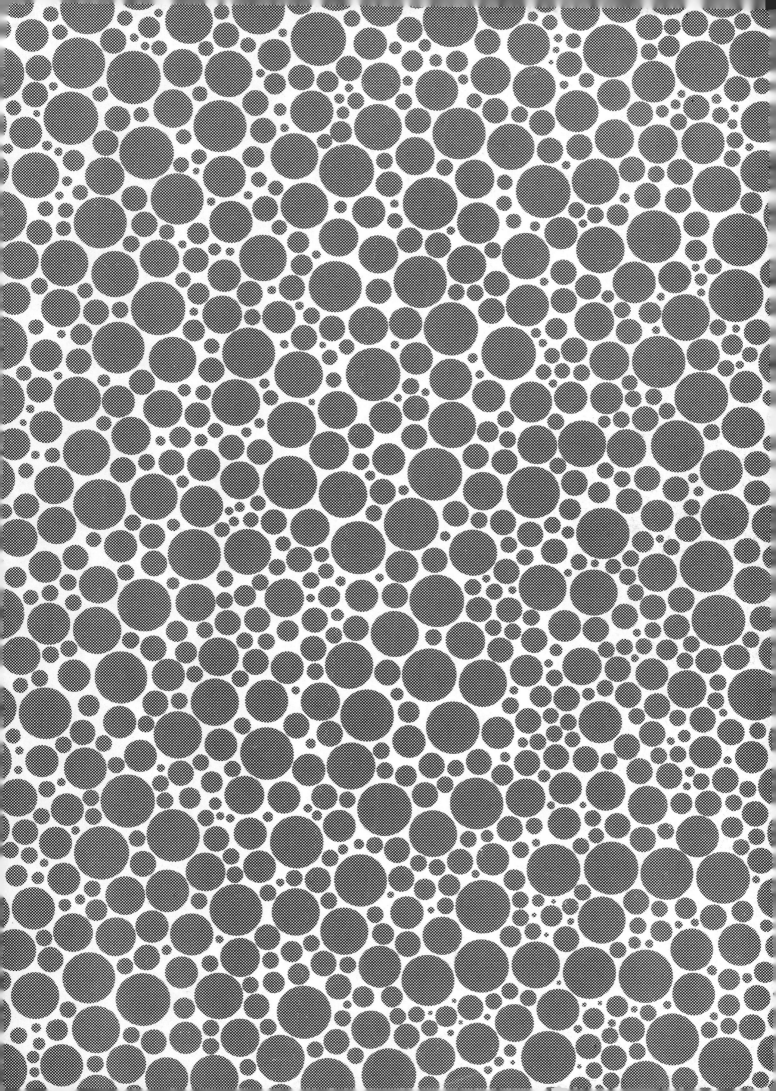

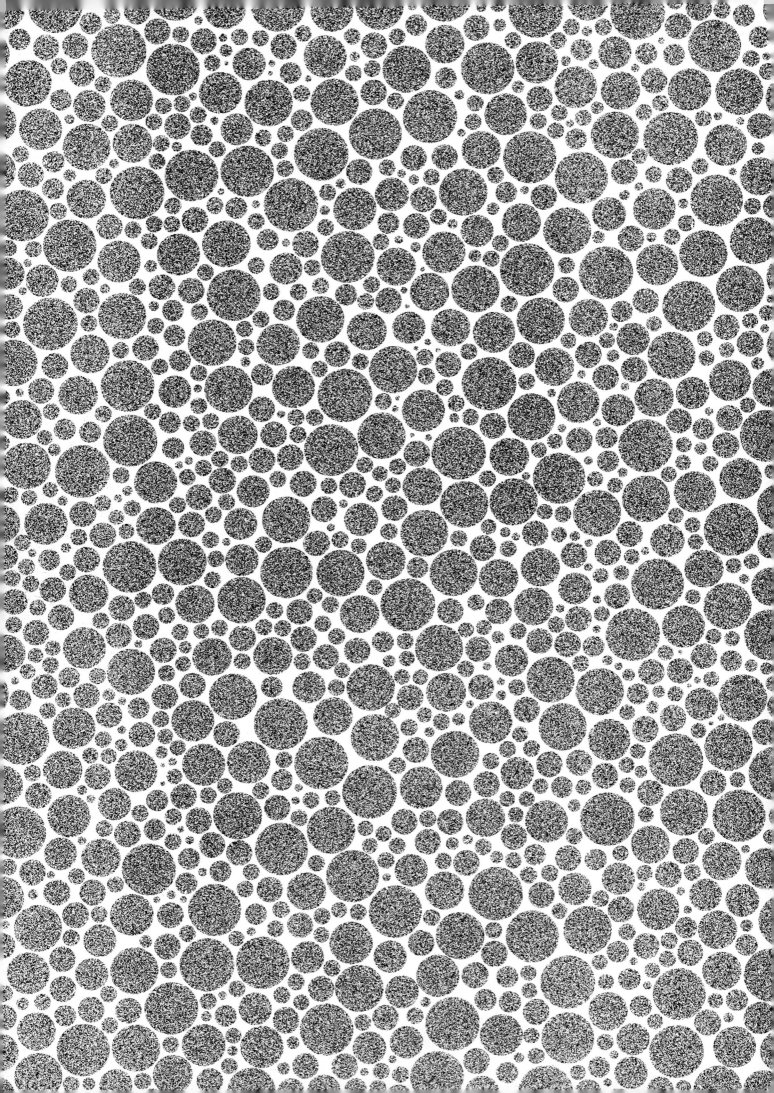

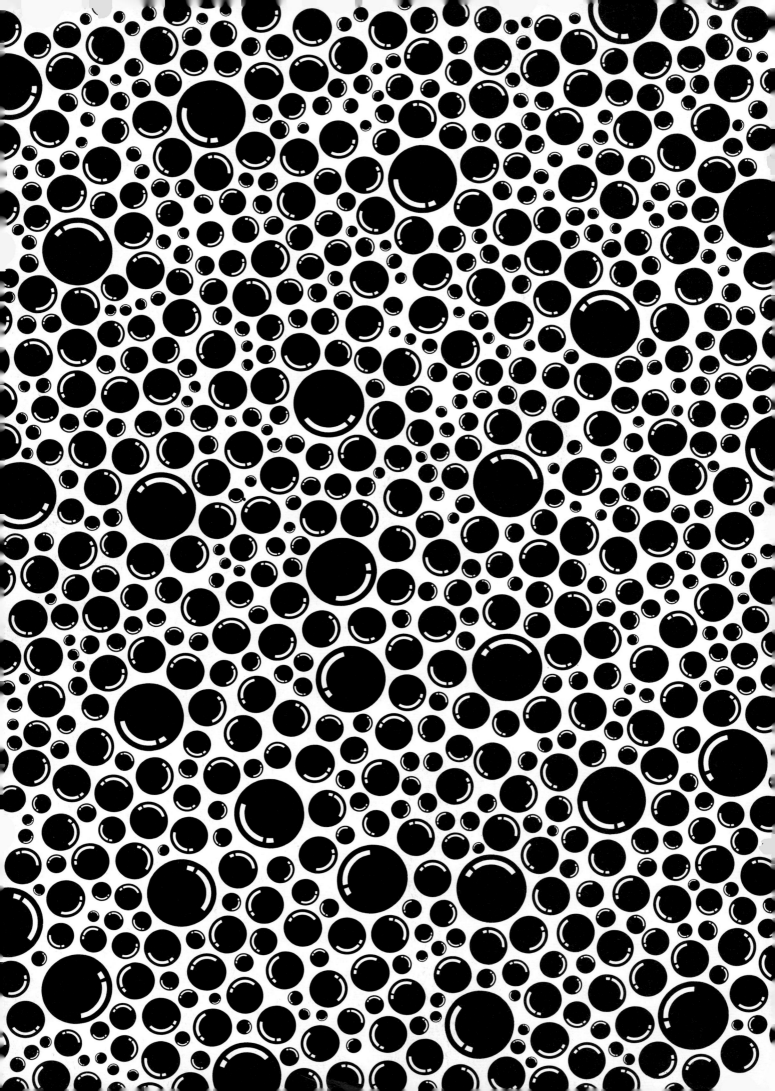

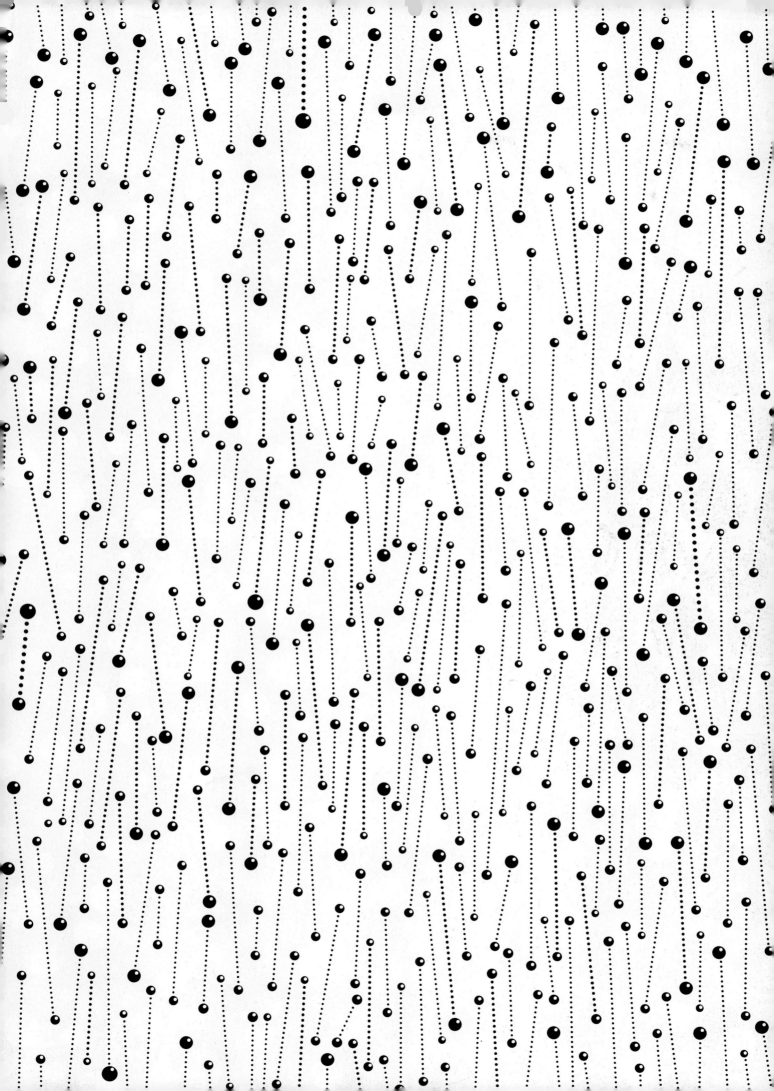

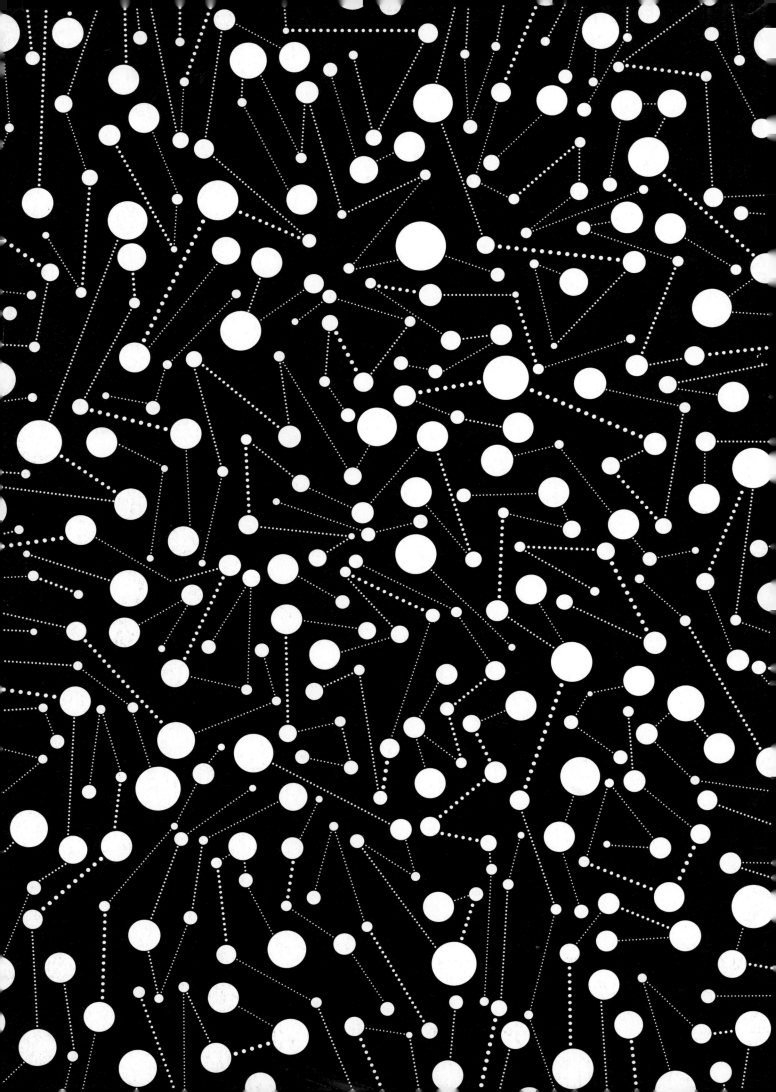

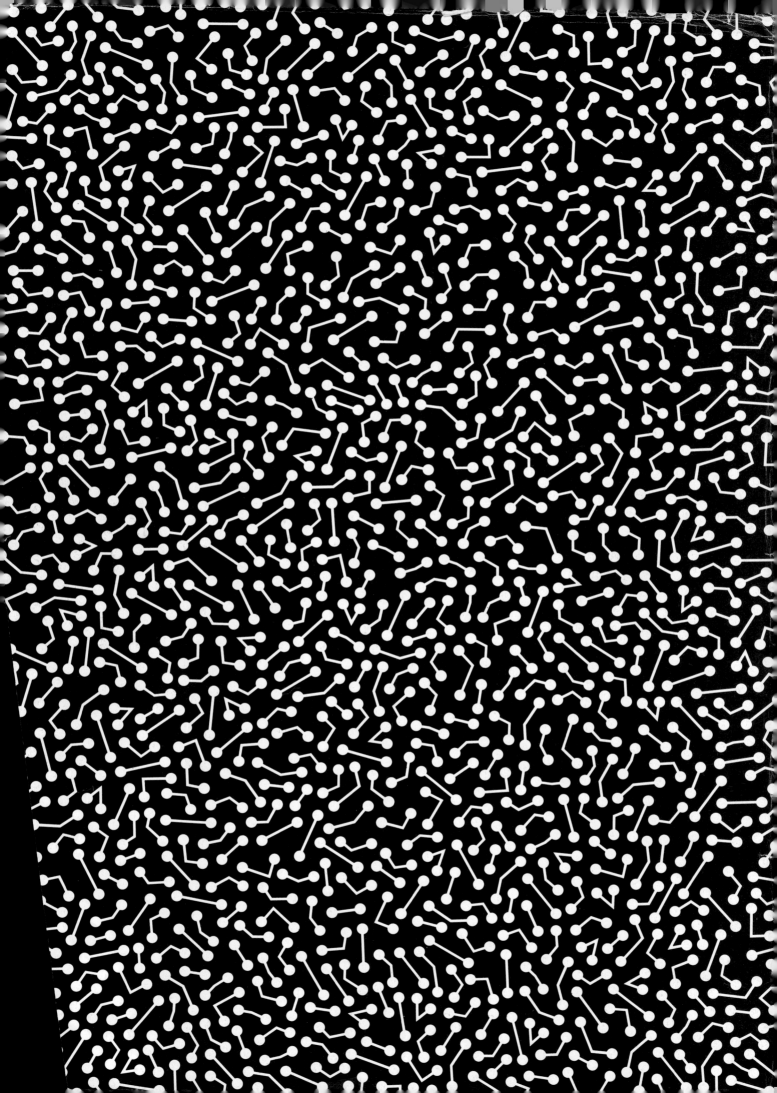

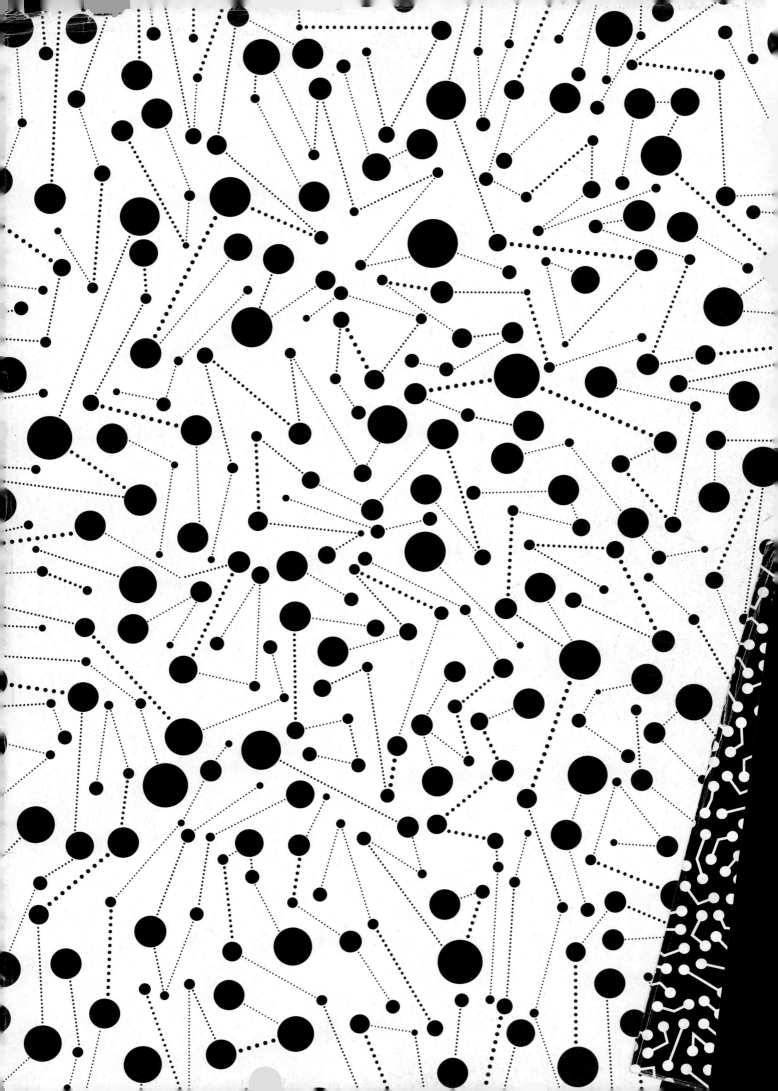

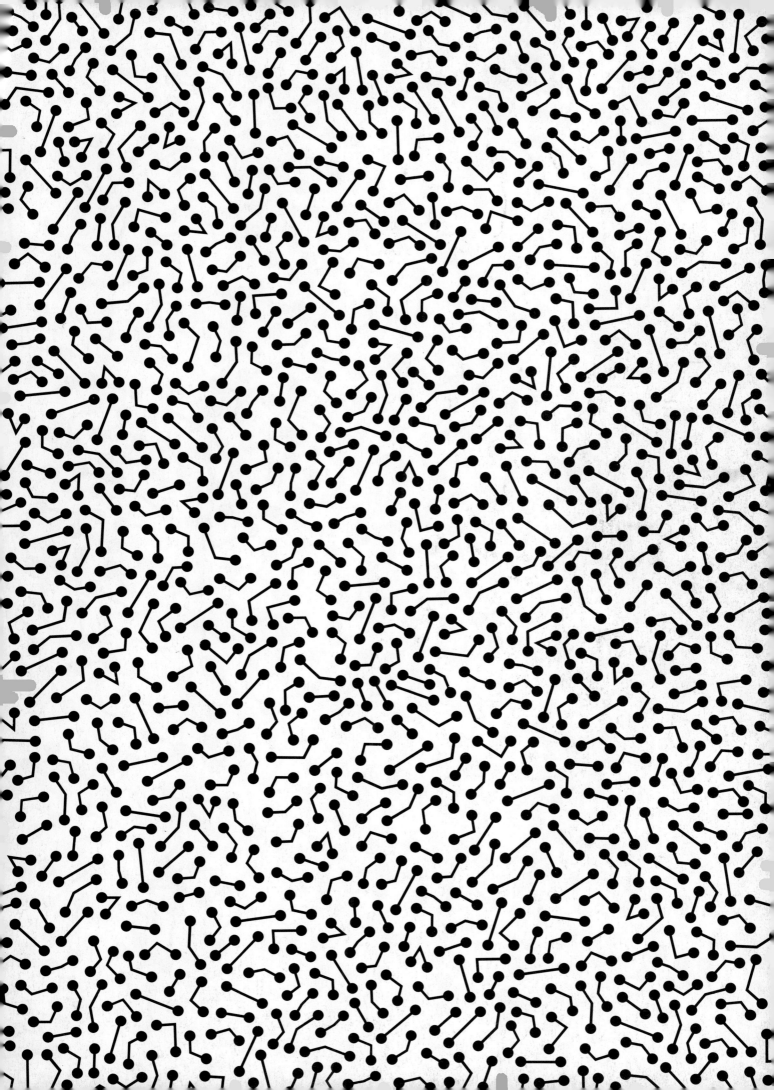

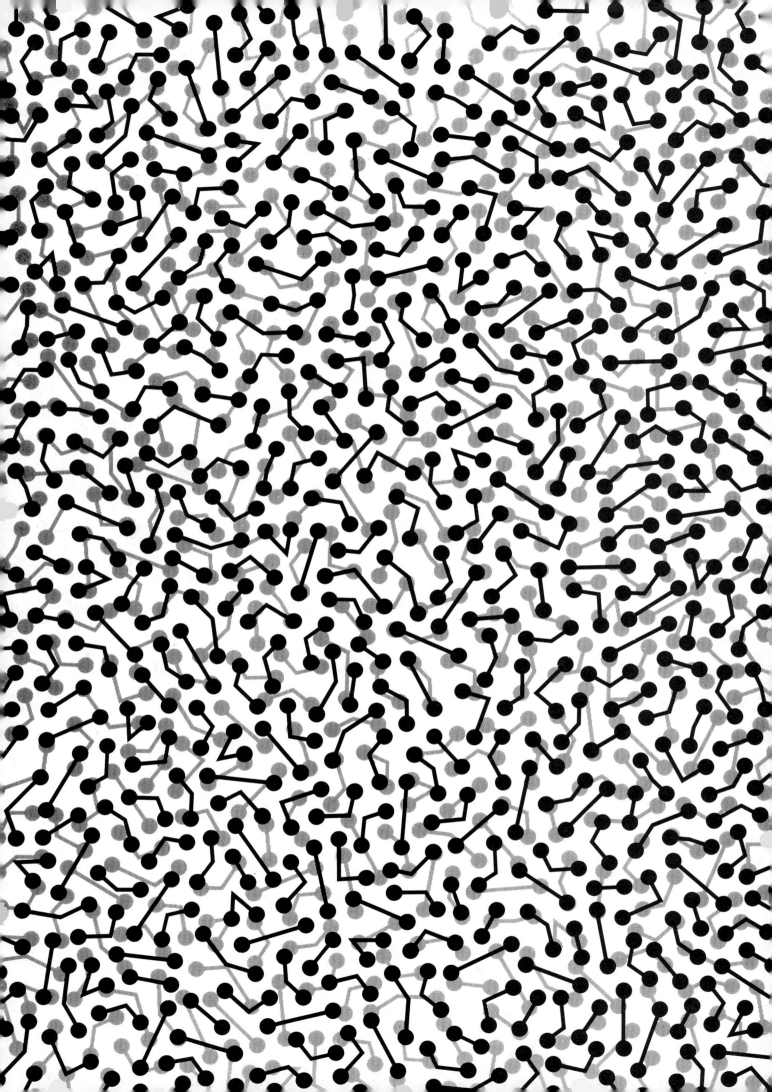

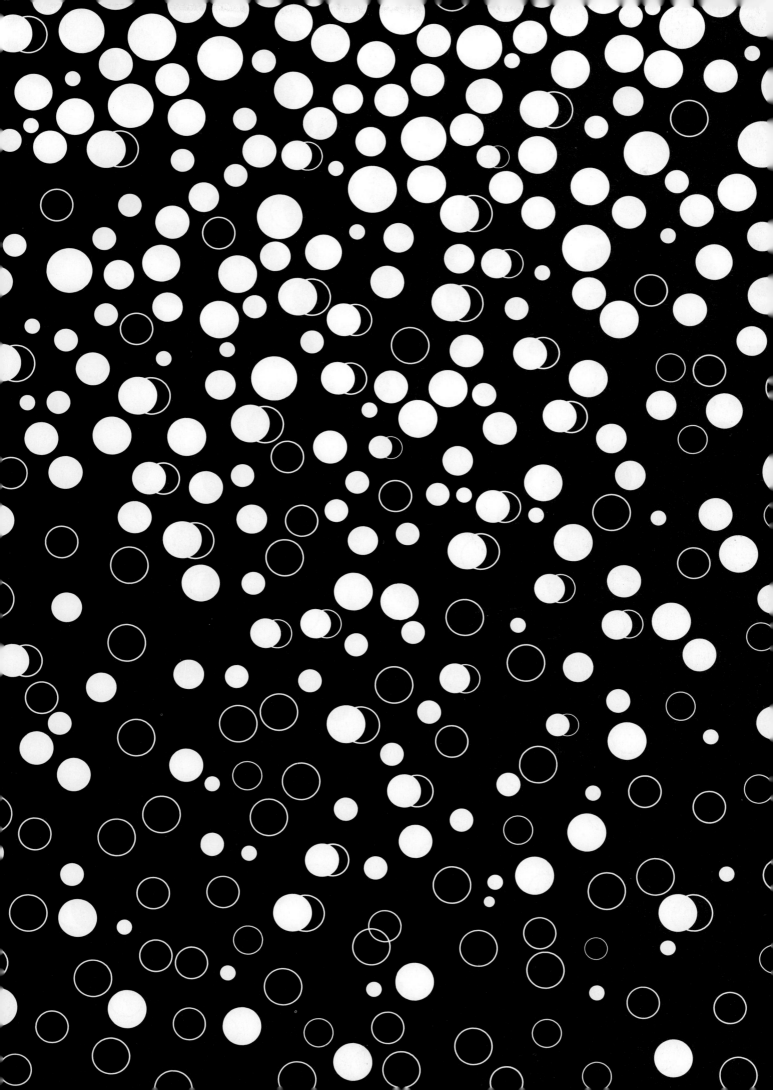

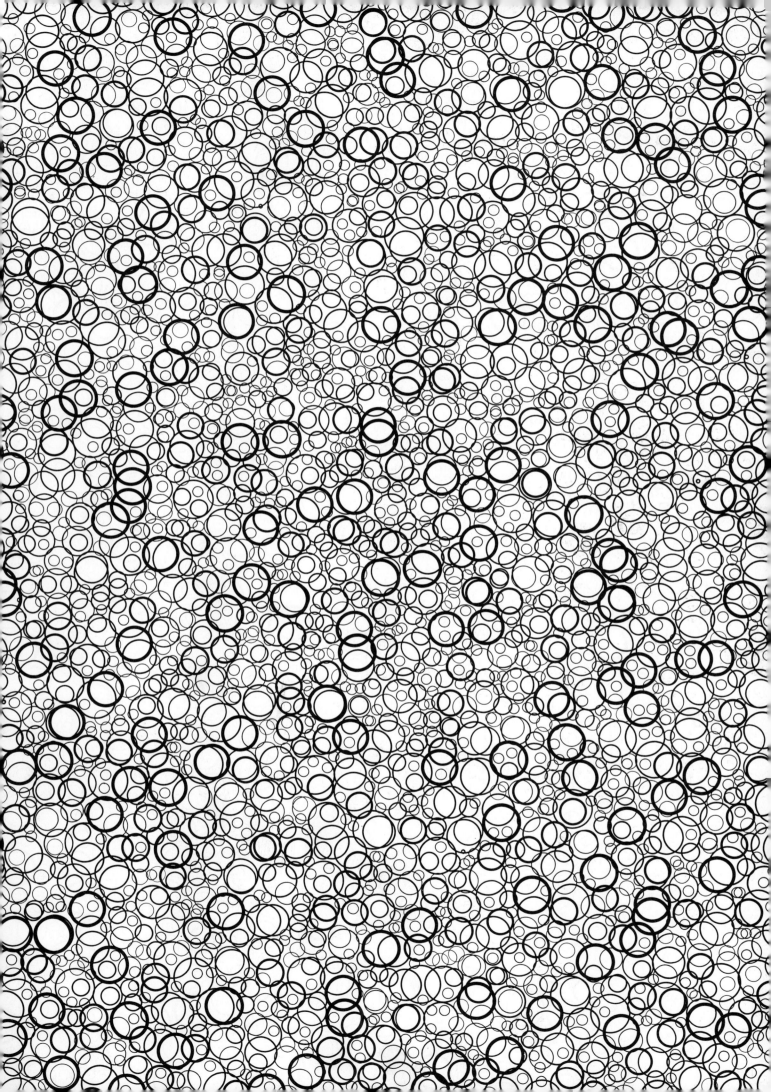

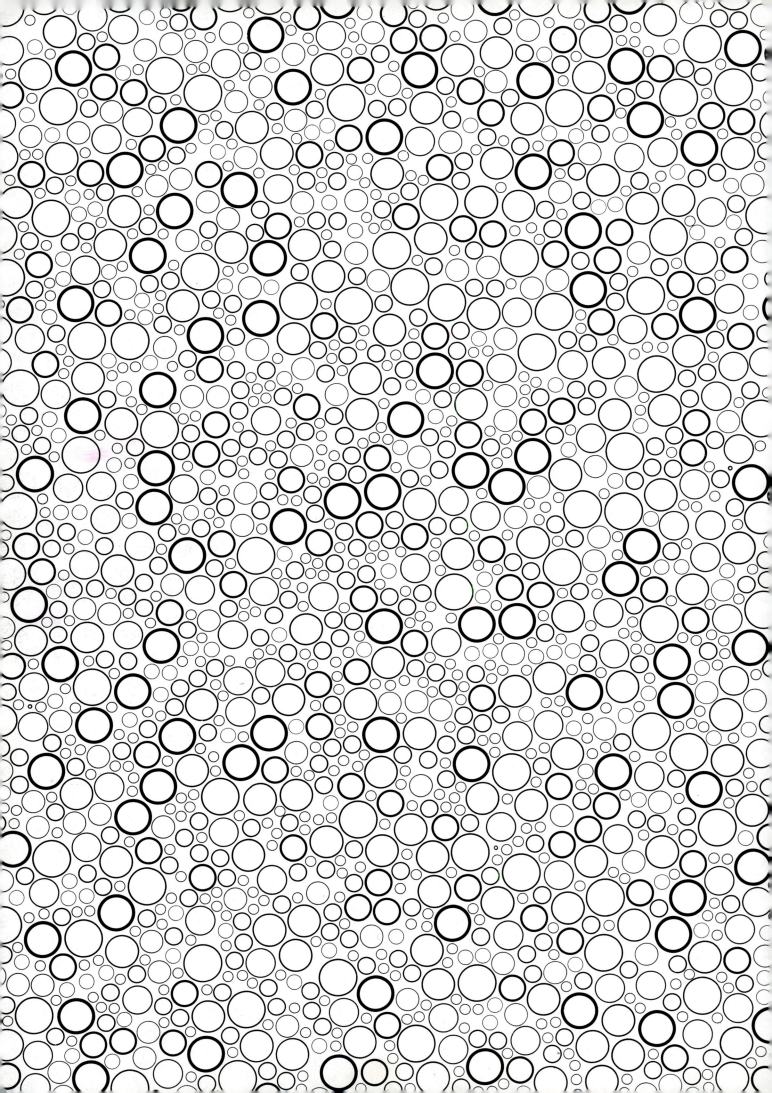

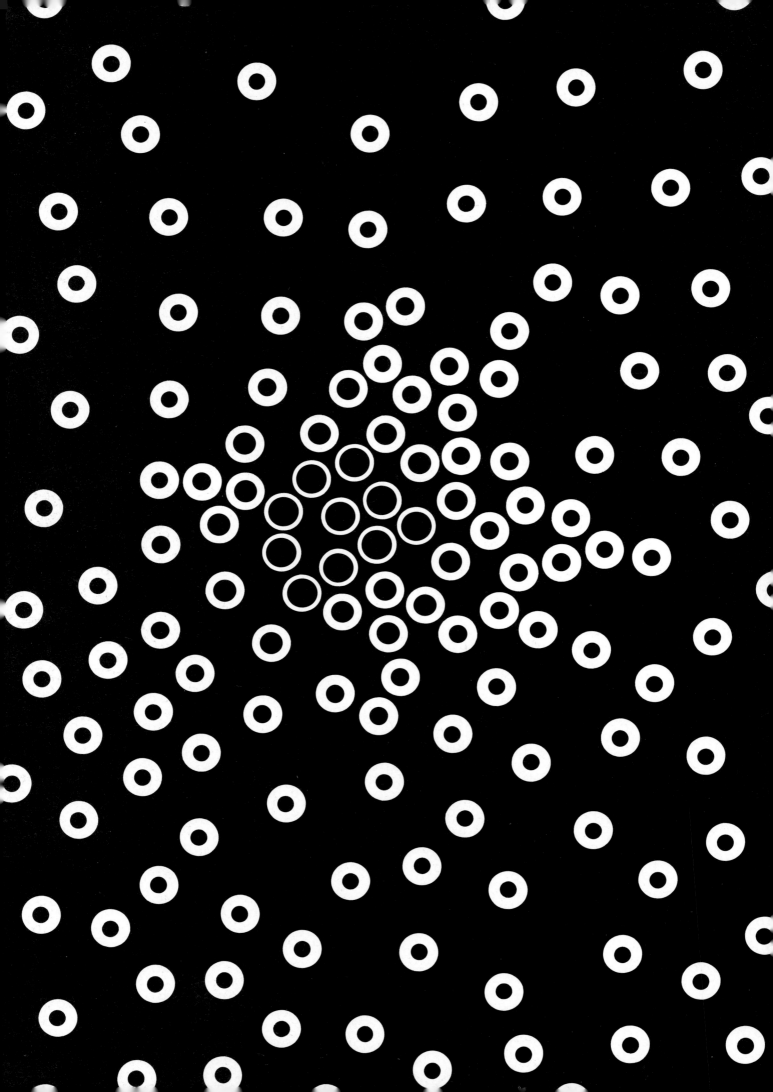

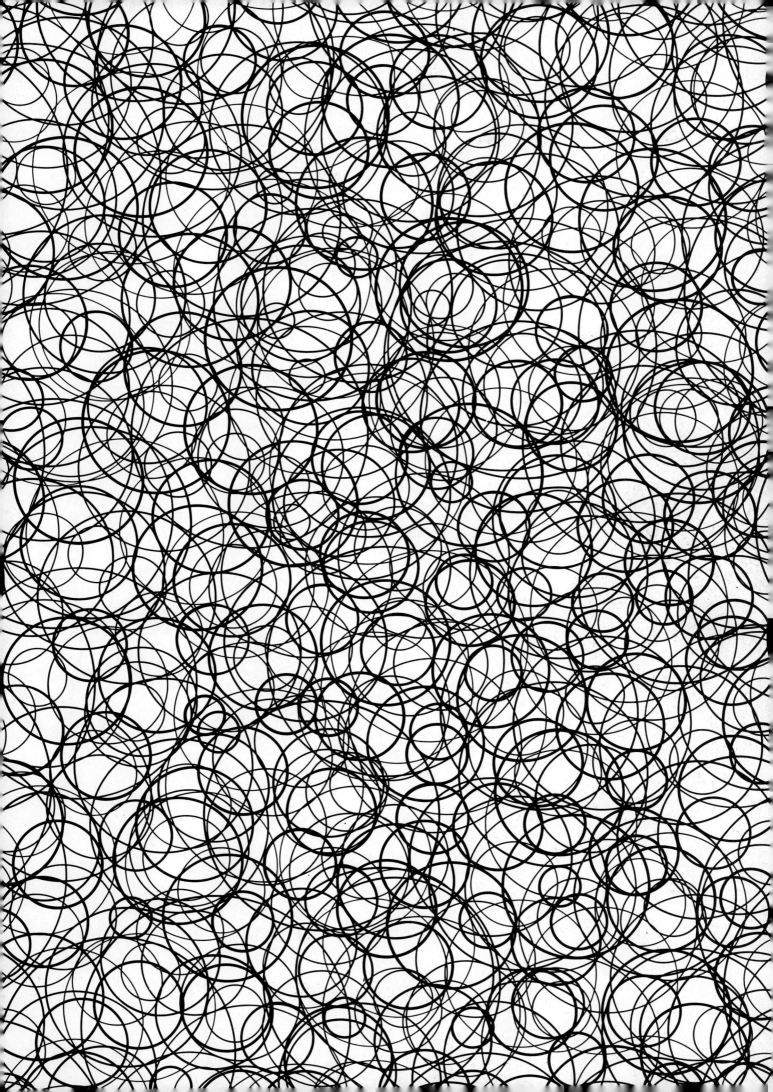

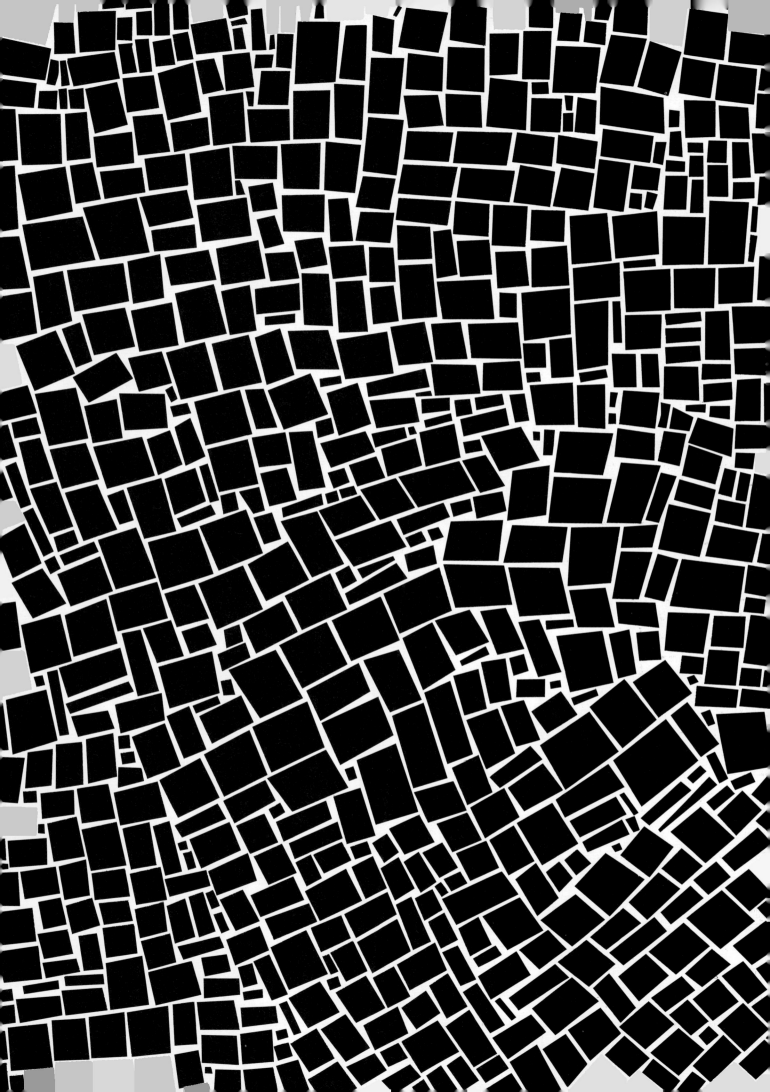

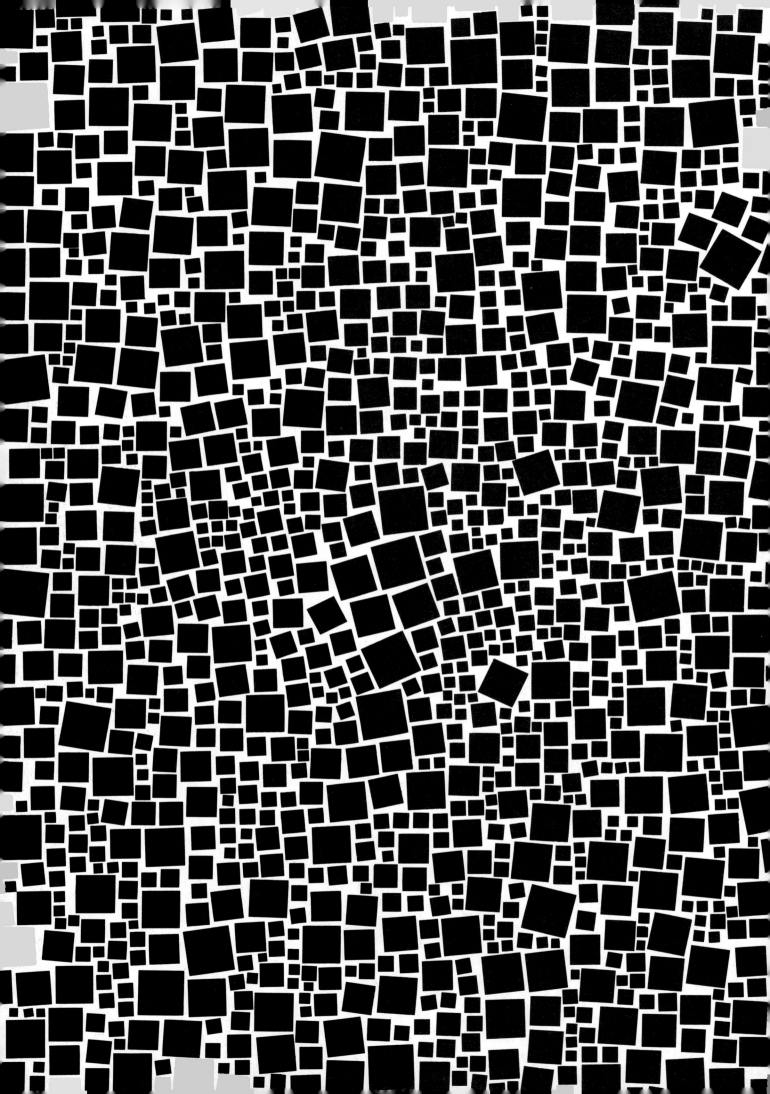

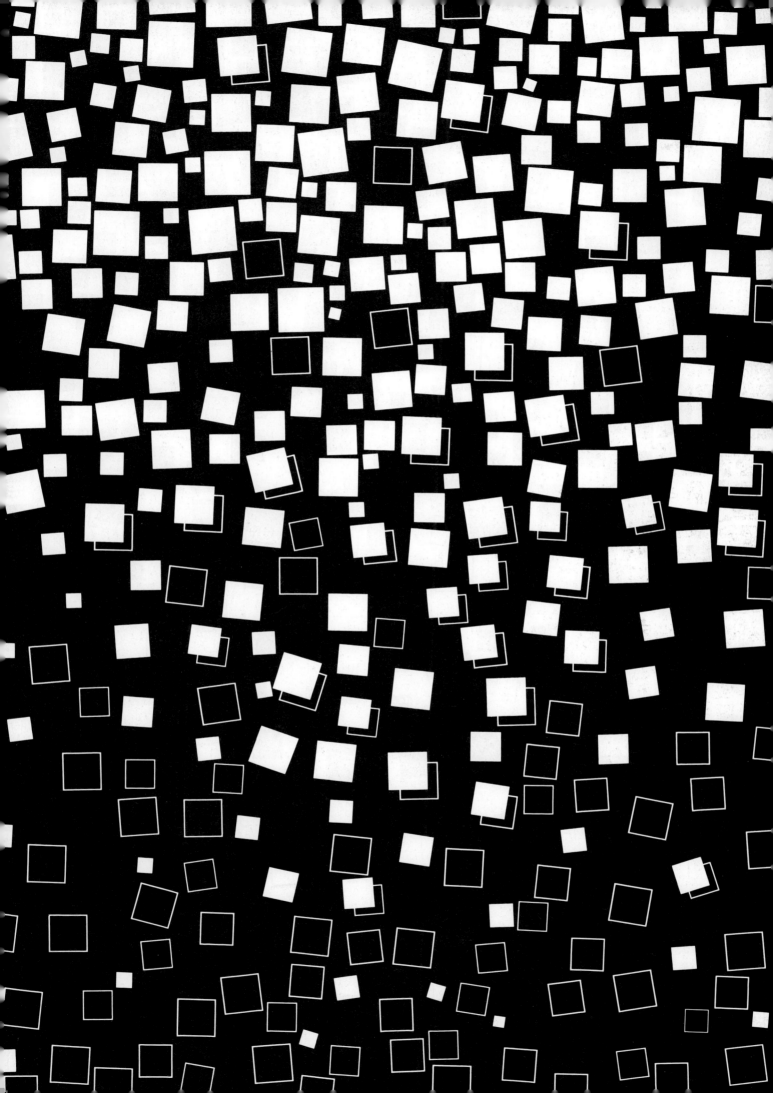

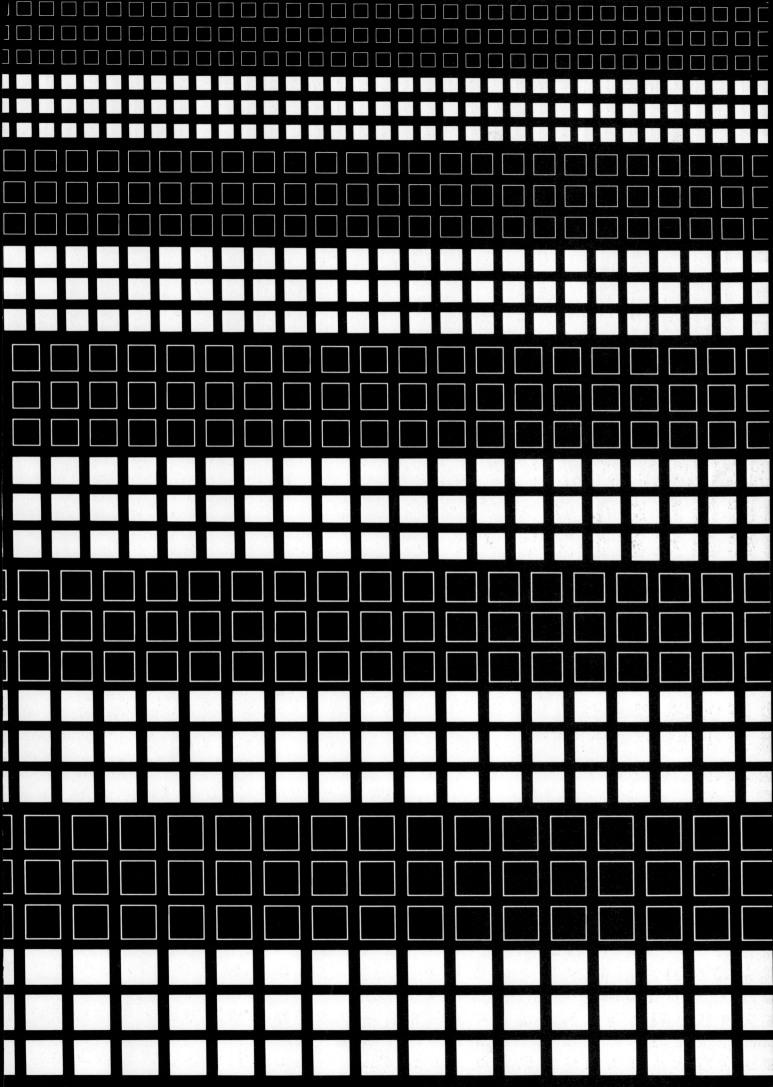

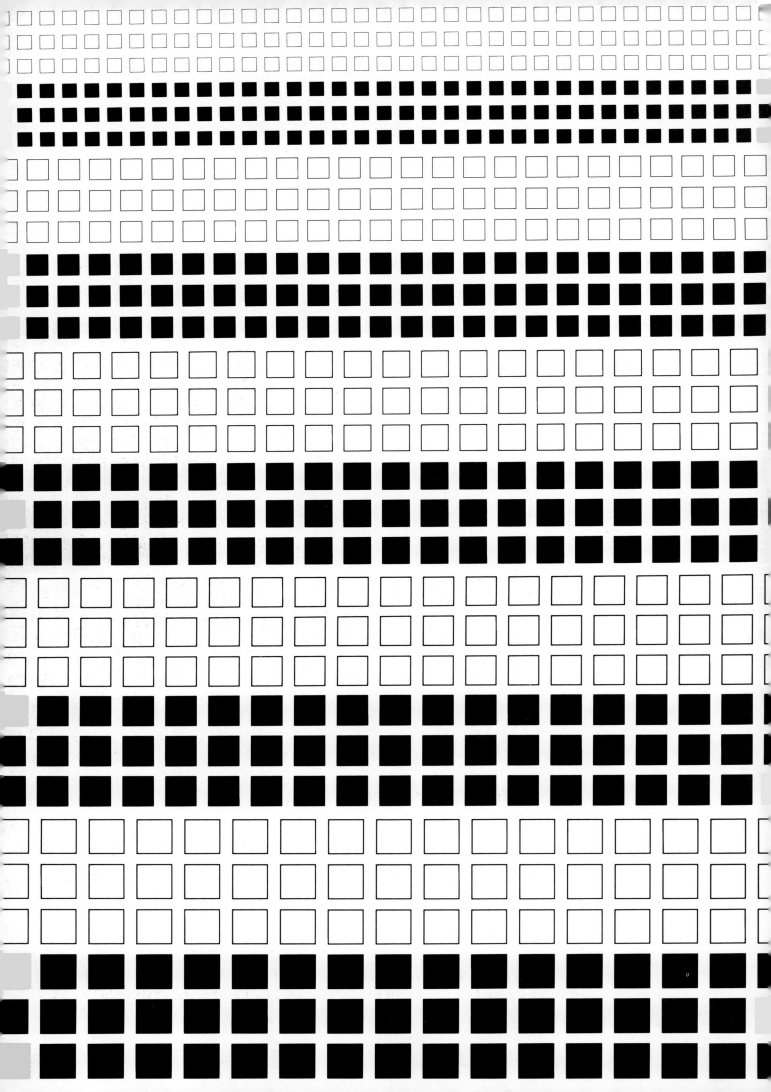

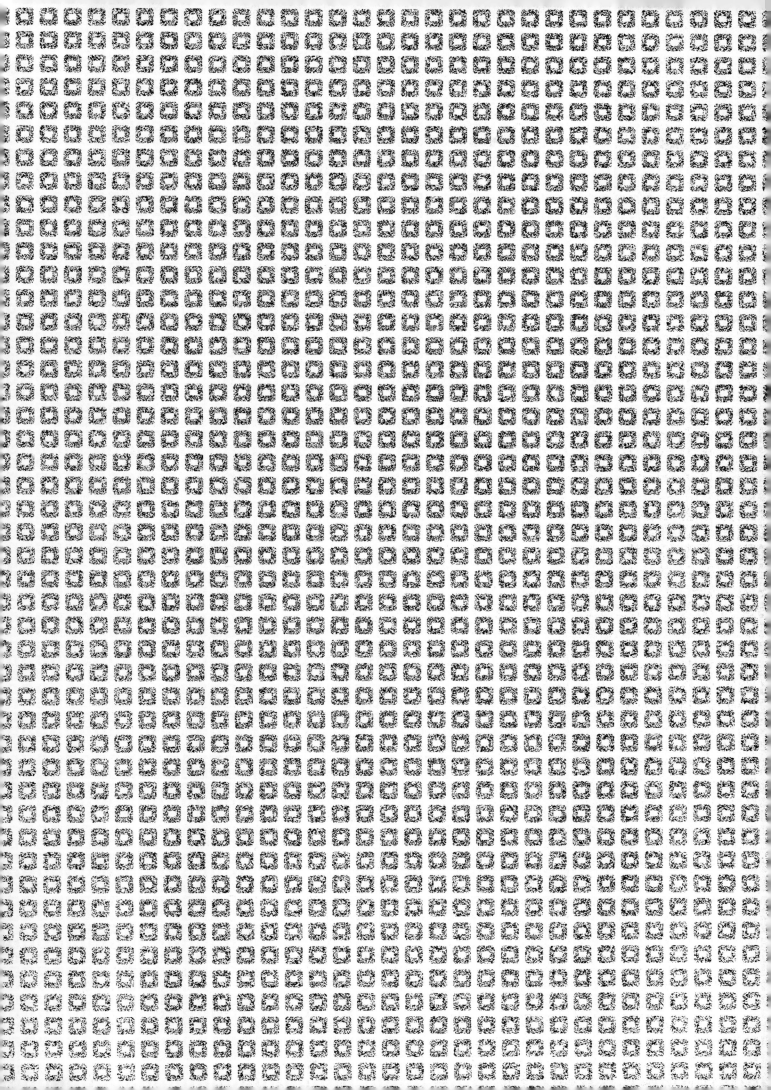

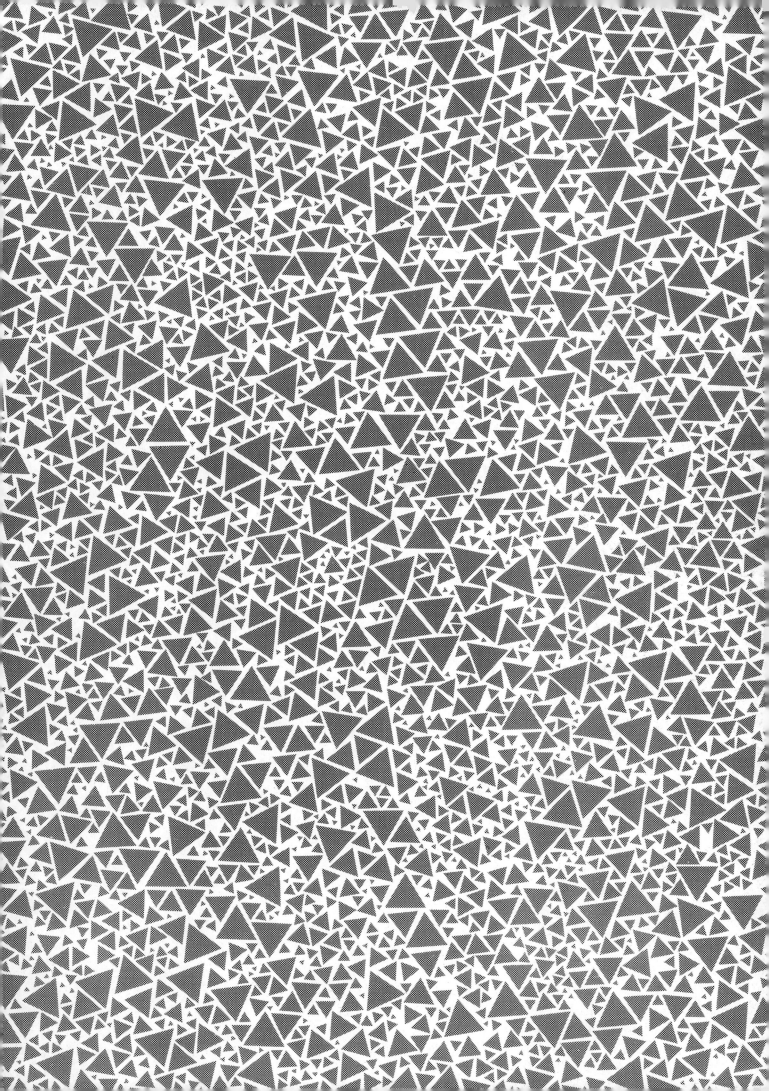

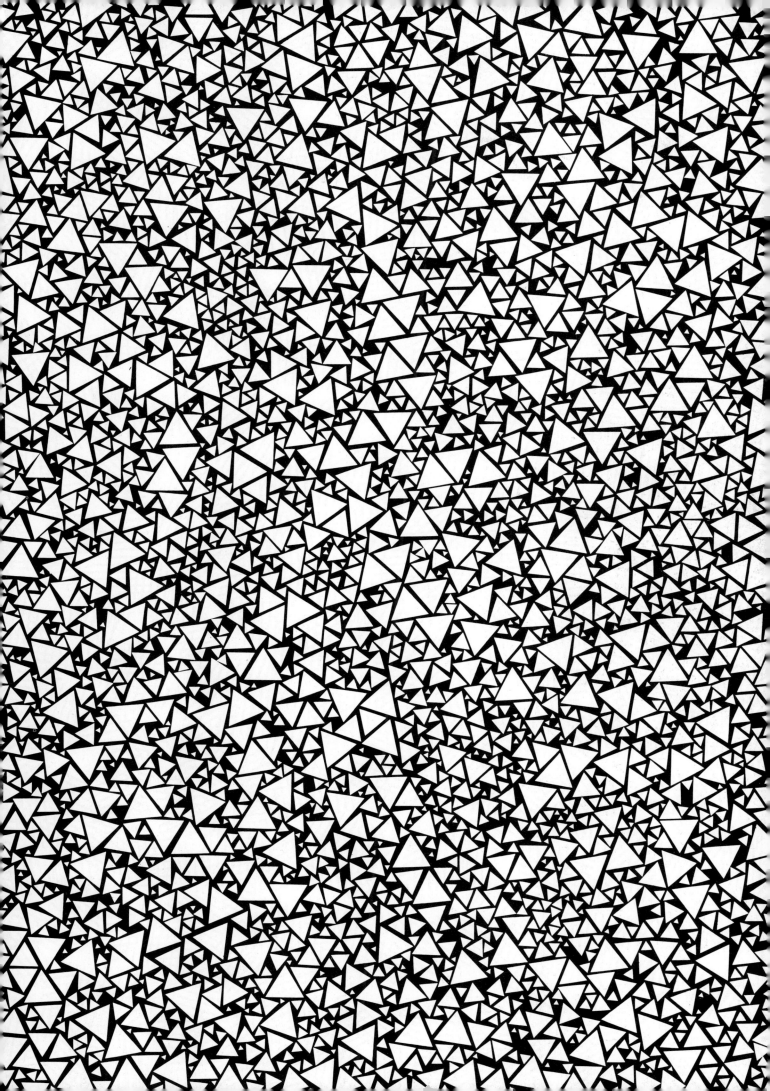

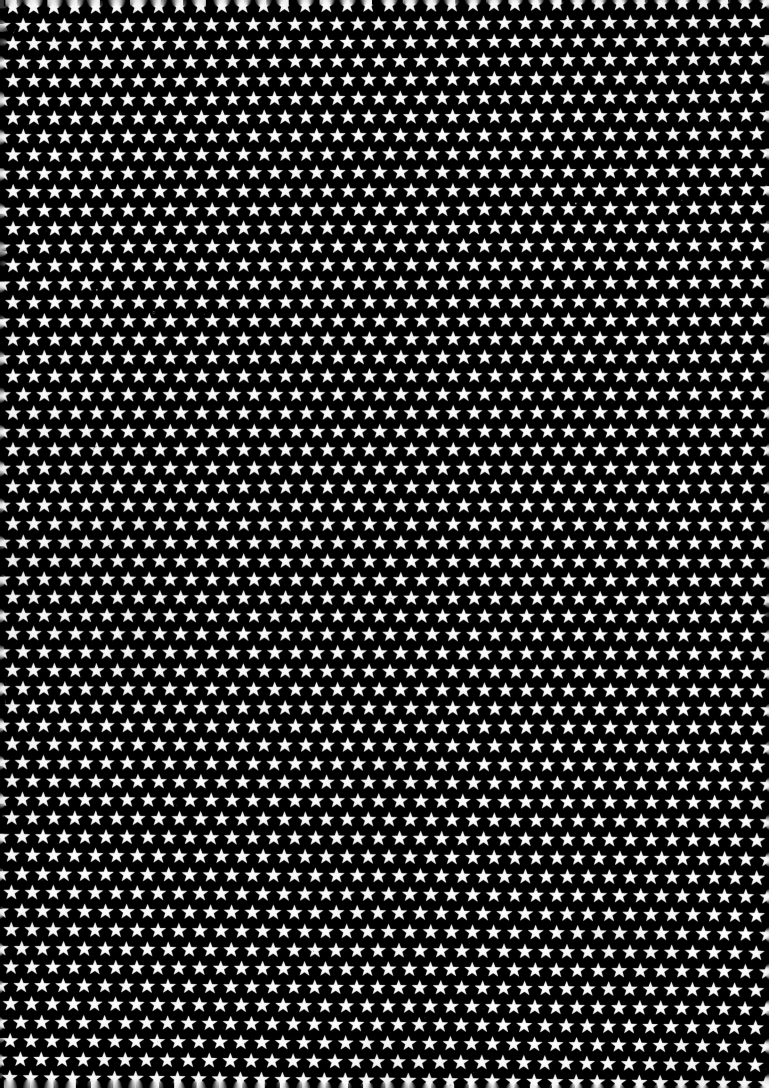

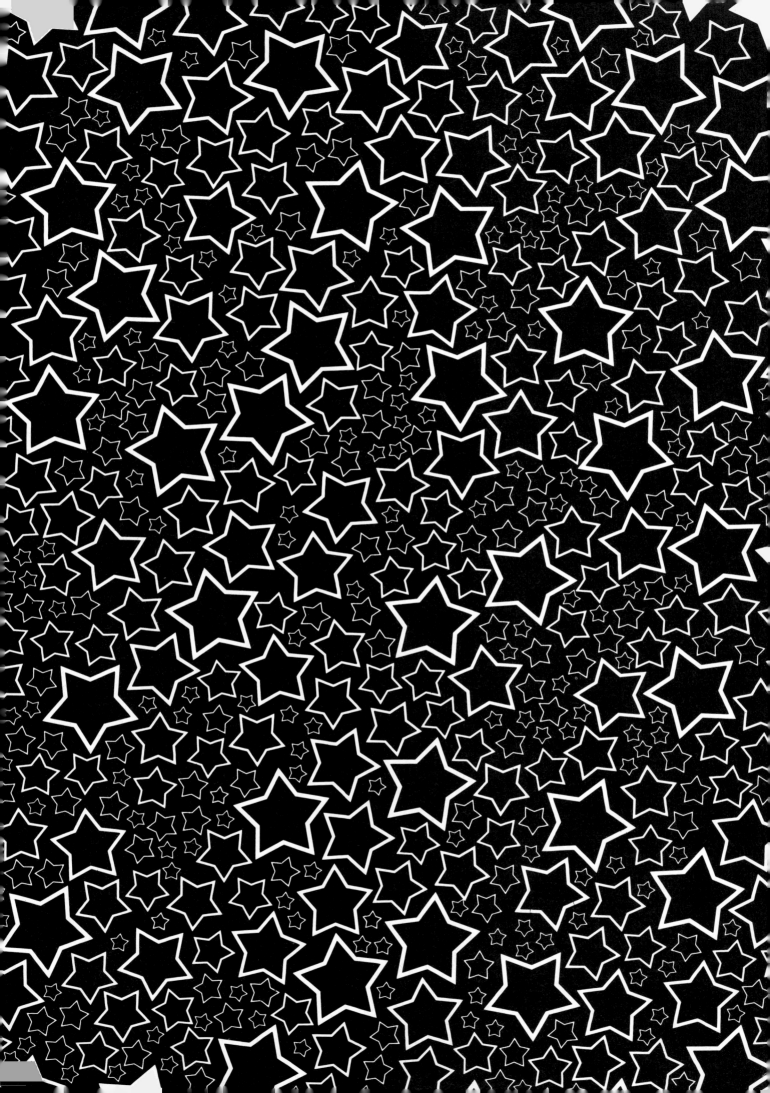

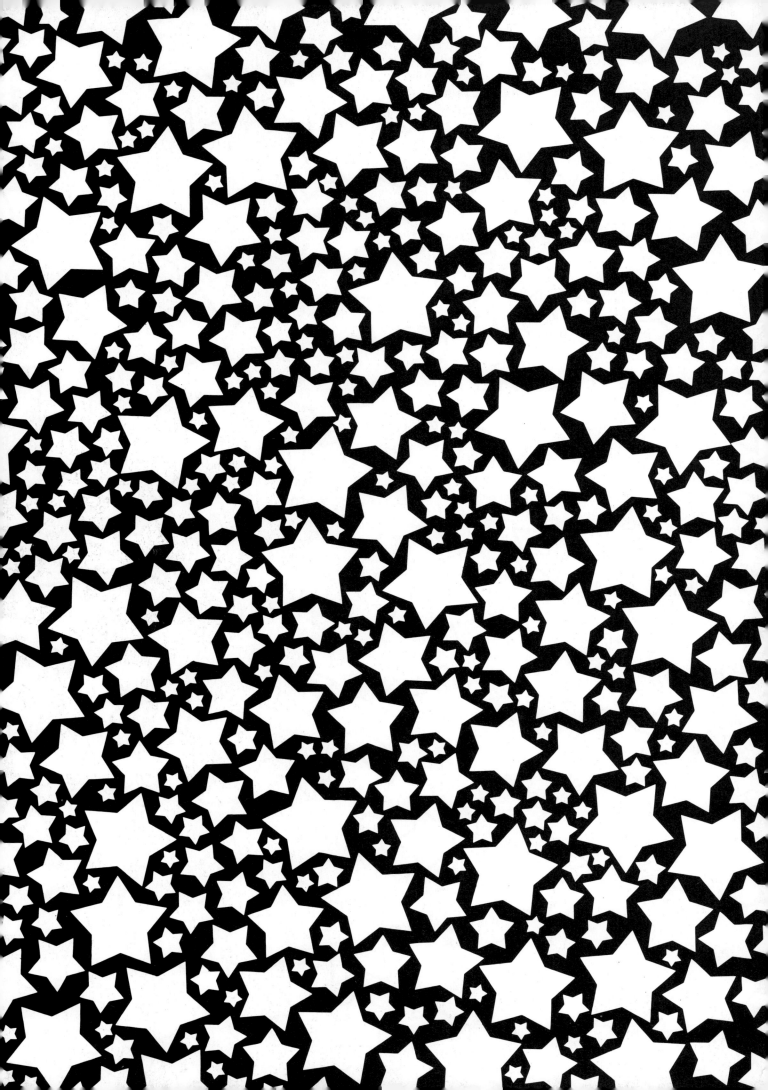

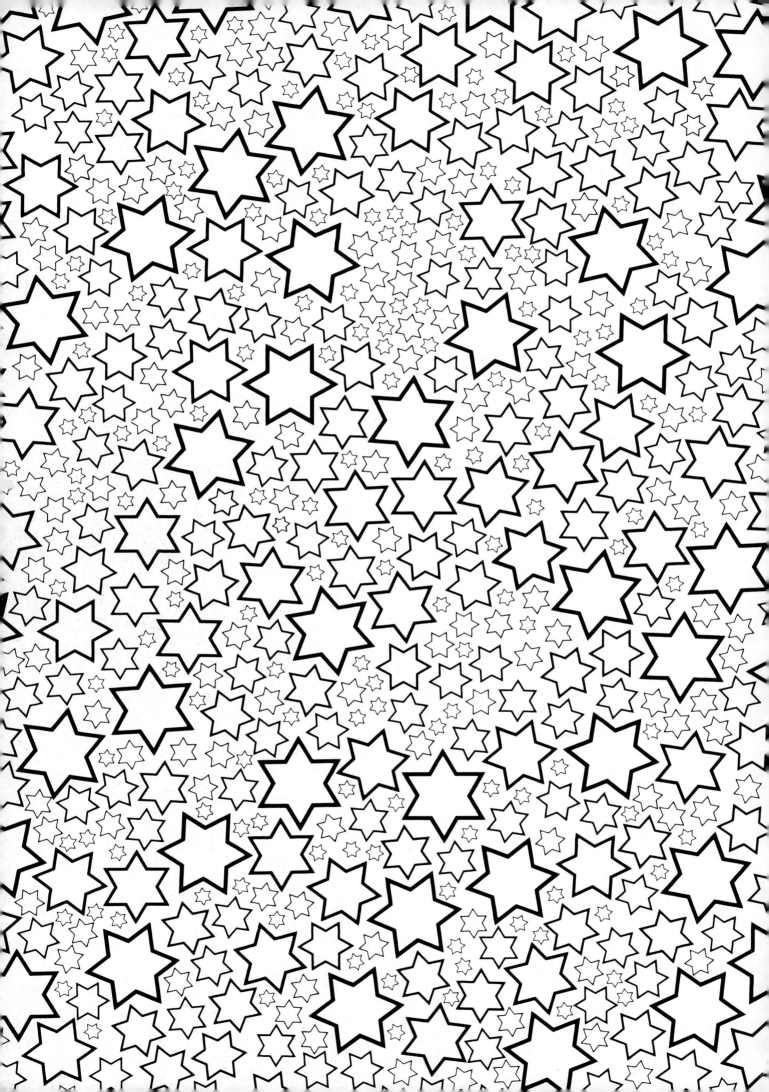

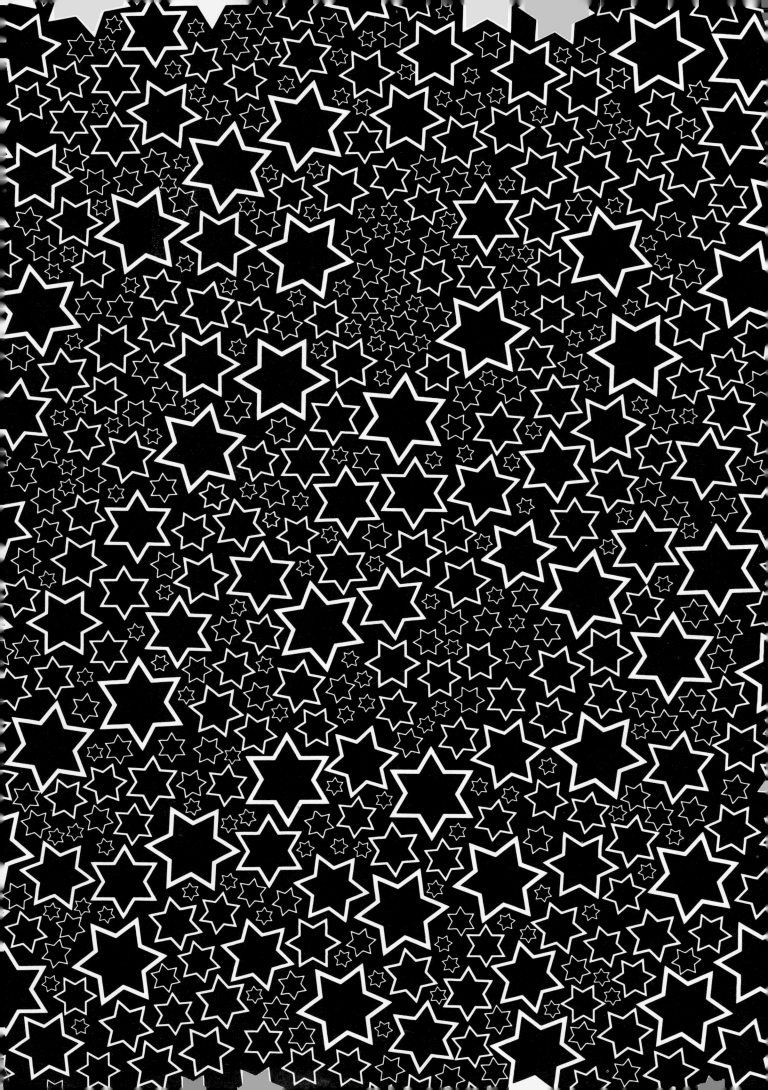

S·PAT'S
SUPER SPECIAL BACKGROUND PATTERN's
BY HIRONORI YASUDA
PINEAPPLE's STUDIO GRAPHIC

ON SALE NOW!

1 DOT
2 STRIPES
3 PAINTINGS
4 CHECKERS
5 COPYS
6 ALPHABETS
7 READERS
8 ANIMALS
9 POPS
10 CROSSINGS

NEXT NUMBER'S

11 GENERATION
12 WARPS
13 SPECKLE
14 GRADATION
15 WAVE
16 MOIRE
17 LOVELY HEART
18 BLOCKS
19 COLLECTORS
20 ZIGZAG

This is a comprehensive collection of patterns used in design work, especially graphic design. The full page designs are easy to use because they can be reproduced using a trescope, or by simply cutting out any pattern you desire. Since so many different patterns are presented you can greatly enhance the range of your design work. In fact, just by leafing through the book, you'll find new inspirations that will improve your own creativity.

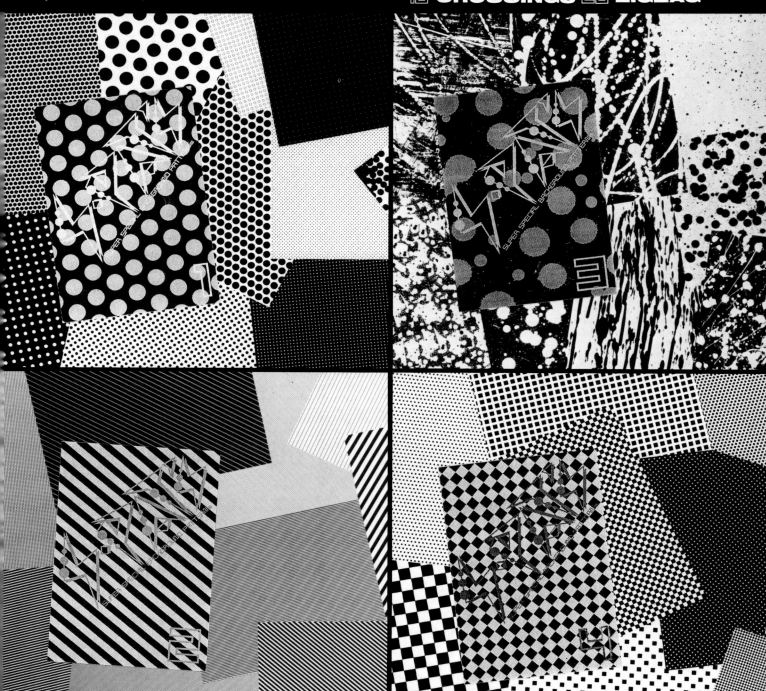

SUPER SPECIAL BACKGROUND PATTERN's
9 POPS

Copyright © 1989 HIRONORI YASUDA by PINEAPPLE's STUDIO GRAPHIC

First printing ▷ APRIL 1989 in Japan

Art direct & Design ▷ HIRONORI YASUDA PINEAPPLE's STUDIO GRAPHIC
Coordinat & Design ▷ KEIKO YASUDA PINEAPPLE's STUDIO GRAPHIC
Plan.Edit.Art work ▷ PINEAPPLE's STUDIO GRAPHIC
207. 1-17-2 Ebisunishi Shibuya-ku Tokyo 150 Japan
TEL:03-770-8615 in FAX
Special thanks ▷ STRAWBERRY's PARTY D+COMPANY STUDIO MINIX
Printing ▷ DAINIPPON PRINTING CO.,LTD. in Japan
Publisher ▷ YOHJIRO NISHII K.D.C CO.,LTD.
K.D.C Staff ▷ CHIE IZUMI K.D.C CO.,LTD.
JUNYA KOSAKA K.D.C CO.,LTD.
Published ▷ THE PATTERN's CONNECTION INTERNATIONAL
PRODUCE By K.D.C CO.,LTD.
1F Daiichikuni bldg., 2-9-12 Hiyakunincho Shinjuku-ku
Tokyo 169 Japan TEL:03-364-1321 FAX:03-367-0135

NIPPAN

WORLD WIDE ▷ Nippon Shuppan Hanbai Inc.
4-3, Kandasurugadai Chiyoda-ku,Tokyo 101 Japan
Tel:03-233-1111 Fax:03-292-8517 Tlx:25627 NIPPAN J
U.S.A., CANADA ▷ Books Nippan Nippon Shuppan Hanbai U.S.A. Inc.
1123 Dominguez Street, Suite 'K'
Carson, California 90746 U.S.A.
Tel:213-604-9701,9702 Fax:213-604-1134
EUROPE ▷ Nippon Shuppan Hanbai Deutschland GmbH
Immermannstr. 45 4000 Düsseldorf. F.R.GERMANY
Tel:0211-360738, 360739 Fax:0211-365617
Tlx:8588795 NSHD D
Nippon Shuppan Hanbai (UK) Ltd.
64 St. Paul's Churchyard London EC4M BAA U.K.
Tel:01-248-4956 Fax:01-489-1171
TAIWAN R.O.C. ▷ RYH Sheng Books
RN 502, 5 fl, Lidye commercial Bldg.
No.22 Nanking W. Road Taipei,Taiwan R.O.C.
Tel:02-571-1016 Fax:02-581-6986
HONG KONG ▷ Hong Kong IPS Inc.
2nd Floor, Shop No.31-33 Admiralty Centre,
Tower One No.18 Harcourt Rd. Hong Kong
Tel:5-294-777 Fax:5-297-170

ISBN4-87708-089-9 C2070

● The owner of this book is authorized to use the pattern's in this book without prior permission from the PINEAPPLE's STUDIO.
● The reproduction of this book in whole or part is prohibited.
● This book's copyright has the PINEAPPLE's STUDIO GRAPHIC.